FENG-SHUI
AND
WESTERN BUILDING CEREMONIES

DERHAM GROVES

Graham Brash, Singapore
and
Tynron Press, Scotland

© Derham Groves, 1991

First published in 1991 by
Graham Brash (Pte) Ltd
227 Rangoon Road
Singapore 0821
and
Tynron Press
Stenhouse, Thornhill
Dumfriesshire DG3 4LD
Scotland

ISBN 9971-49-244-X (Graham Brash)
      1-85645-012-6 (Tynron Press)

Cover design by Peter Jones, London
Typeset by Quaser Technology (Pte) Ltd
Printed in Singapore by Chong Moh Offset (Pte) Ltd

Contents

Preface

I began studying architecture at the Gordon Institute of Technology in 1976, the same year that Phillip Gibbs started teaching there. He had just spent the previous five years at the Universiti Sains Malaysia, so I was among the first to hear his lectures on the Malay building process. His lectures about Malay building ceremonies fascinated me in particular, and I began studying building ceremonies more widely.

I wish to thank the following people especially for their encouragement and help: Khoo Ping Tiang, Huey Groves, Leon Van Schaik, Greg Missingham, Yi-Fu Tuan, Peter Corrigan, Ru Chi Li, Danny Gu Zhong Liang, Evelyn Lip, Lin Yun, Ma Yan Chow, Dean Wakefield, Austin McLean, Linda Liew, Yvonne Jong, Joan Nassauer, Peter Downton, and my students of architecture at RMIT.

Derham Groves
Brunswick West
1991

Feng-shui
and
Western Building Ceremonies

For Ethel and Lewis Groves,
my Mum and Dad.

Foreword

In the modern world, we see buildings — modest and grand — sprouting up everywhere. Such activity arouses unease as much as it does pride. Nature, we feel, is overwhelmed by human ingenuity, power and greed. A lay-person, as he approaches a building project, is so overwhelmed by the roar of machines, the yawning hole in the ground, the towering cranes and the rapid rise of scaffolds of brutal strength that he may forget the creative thrust of architecture, its age-old function to build a world that can satisfy a people's spiritual as well as material needs.

Contemporary man and woman, blindly confident in their command of technological power, also tend to forget that buildings are mental as well as physical realities, that they are sustained not only by steel girders and concrete but also by edifices of human discourse, ceremony and ritual. We all know of the notorious example of Pruitt-Igoe, an award-winning public housing project in St. Louis, Missouri, that had to be demolished only twenty years after it was built. What happened? The physical structure itself was sound, and yet it could not 'stand up' because it lacked totally a corresponding structure of human words and gestures — the formal and informal acts of mutual concern.

A building is, in a fundamental sense, a shelter. It keeps out hostile forces, whether human or natural. But it is also, in another fundamental sense that we now neglect, an intermediary. It mediates between insiders and outsiders: its partitions and spaces allow for graduated relationships among human beings. To be civilised is to have these graduated, ceremonial relationships. The building also mediates between nature 'outside' and human beings 'inside': it mediates rather than separates, and this mediation is often expressed as a series of correspondences between external nature and the character of the built environment at different scales — city, house and room. The reality of these correspondences is not self-evident; it has to be made vivid by ceremony.

If a reader agrees with what I have just sketched, he will want to know more, he will want documentation, and he will wish for further and deeper insights. Here the reader is in luck, for I can think of no better contemporary guide than this book by Derham Groves, an architect and student of culture who will examine with him the architectural and ceremonial practices of Malaysia and show him that, though some of these practices may seem premodern and quaint, they are nevertheless expressive of a widespread human belief and need. Mr. Groves explores ways of thought — structures of feeling — in such diverse places as, besides Malaysia, Minnesota (USA) in the nineteenth century, premodern Europe, Sherlock Holmes' Baker Street lodgings and modern Australia. He succeeds in demonstrating that if we want to live in a humanised world rather than in some kind of material shell, we need to be repeatedly reminded of the fact that we are not just clever animals but also creatures or words and gesture, dialogue and ceremony.

Yi-Fu Tuan
J.K. Wright and Vilas Professor
University of Wisconsin, Madison
1991

1. Feng-shui

Introduction

A team of American scientists visited a remote village in China to try to discover why so many twins were born there. They carried out lots of tests but found nothing unusual. Then an old lady approached them and drew their attention to two lofty mountains in the distance. This, she said, was why the villagers produced so many twins.

Many Chinese believe that powerful spirits inhabit the landscape. Living in a place inhabited by good spirits brings such things as good luck, long life, increased wealth and high social standing. Living in a place inhabited by bad spirits brings the opposite. The ancient Chinese observed what conditions attracted good and bad spirits and encoded this information in a highly complex scientific and magical system of divination called 'kan-yu' (the science of heaven and earth), and subsequently 'feng- shui' (wind and water). *Figure 1.* The origin of feng-shui dates back to antiquity, and evidence shows that as far back as three thousand years ago government residences and imperial palaces were built according to feng-shui principles. Feng-shui is still used to find lucky sites for towns and buildings (dwellings for the living), and cemeteries and graves (dwellings for the dead). Innovations to feng-shui have been minor, and modern-day practices date back to the Sung dynasty (A.D. 960-1126).

Figure 1

Most Chinese have some knowledge of feng-shui, but usually it is not very deep. In **A Winter in North China** (published in 1892), Rev. T.M. Morris writes: "You everywhere meet with evidences of [feng-shui] but, however carefully you inquire, you fail to get any very intelligible definition or description of it."[1] In general, this has been my experience too. For example, one Chinese architecture student from Deakin University explained feng-shui thus:

"The Chinese believe that a person and the place where he lives should be compatible, which is determined by a Chinese temple medium. If they are compatible there is a feast to thank the gods and the temple medium. The temple medium also blesses the foundations of the house by burning paper charms and sprinkling the ashes around the house to protect it from evil spirits. When the house is finished, a charm is hung above the front door to keep evil spirits out of the house."

Many Chinese consult a feng-shui expert, known as a 'feng-shui xian-sheng' (Mr. Feng-shui), or a geomancer who has devoted his life to the study and practice of feng-shui. A geomancer usually charges a fee for his advice. In 1983 a well known geomancer from Hong Kong charged about twenty-five cents for every square foot of land he examined while searching for a suitable site. However, in 1987 some geomancers in Hong Kong charged twelve dollars and fifty cents per square foot. In areas where a geomancer is often hard to come by, in parts of East Malaysia for example, a Chinese priest or temple medium will often give feng-shui advice, sometimes free of charge. While many Chinese regard geomancers as oracles, capable of solving the mysteries of heaven and earth, many also regard them as charlatans, who predict results so far in the future that their efficacy cannot be measured truly.

The practice of feng-shui is banned by the Communist Party in the People's Republic of China - a legacy of the Cultural Revolution of the 1960's. In 1983 the leader of a commune in Guangdong was expelled from the Party for participating in a ceremony to 'drive ghosts' from the site of a new office building. Clanging gongs and beating drums, he led commune officials in a noisy procession to the site where they fired pistols in the air and set off firecrackers. He also hired a geomancer to help design the building and calculate the best time to start construction. Feng-shui is still practised fairly widely in the Chinese country-side, despite this ban. It also flourishes in other countries, wherever Chinese people live.

In 1988 I did a short course on Chinese architecture at the Southeast

University, in Nanjing. I was particularly looking forward to the lecture on feng- shui, but it turned out to be rather disappointing, because my teacher's knowledge of the subject came directly from a book written by an American! Why is feng-shui not taught to architecture students in China (or the rest of the world, for that matter) when acupuncture, which in several respects is analogous to feng-shui, is taught to medical students?

I believe feng-shui is important for several reasons: it makes a place special or meaningful, which in turn helps to foster a bond between person and place; it permits people to actively participate in the building process; it reflects people's values and aspirations; it holds out various rewards and penalties; it has a mystical side and a practical side; it is practised very widely; many cultures practise systems of divination which are very similar in character to feng-shui; and it is a powerful design tool.

Some factors which influence feng-shui

A geomancer must take many factors into account when assessing the feng-shui of a place. Yang and yin, the five elements, the eight trigrams, qi and sha qi are among the most important factors to be considered.

In Taoist metaphysics yang and yin are two antithetical but comple-mentary forces of nature, which are often represented by a symbol that looks like two tadpoles placed head to tail. The Chinese classify things by yang and yin. Yang is male, yin is female; yang is light, yin is dark; yang is active, yin is passive; and so on. A geomancer searches for a site where the forces of yang and yin are balanced. The luckiest site is where there is a transition from yang to yin or from yin to yang, and where the surroundings combine both yang and yin characteristics in the proper proportion, which is three-fifths yang to two-fifths yin. For example, the Ming tombs near Beijing are located just where the valley floor begins to turn into mountain slopes. The yang and yin of a house must also be delicately balanced. It is unwise to place a stove right next to a well, for example, because the water in the well is too yin and the fire in the stove is too yang.

The ancient Chinese believed that wood, fire, earth, metal and water were the fundamental elements of matter. These five elements produced one another in an endless cycle: wood produced fire, fire produced earth, earth produced metal, metal produced water, and water produced wood. They also destroyed one another in an endless cycle: wood destroyed earth, earth destroyed water, water destroyed fire, fire destroyed metal, and metal destroyed wood. This meant that metal nails, for example, were not used in traditional Chinese buildings because 'metal destroyed wood'.

The idea of endless, cyclical destruction is also the basis of 'Paper-Stone-Scissors', which is a very popular game among Chinese children as well as adults. In this game the palm of the hand represents a sheet of paper, a closed fist represents a stone, and two fingers represent a pair of scissors. On the count of three, each player makes whichever of these gestures he chooses, and the winner is decided as follows: paper wraps stone, so paper wins over stone; stone is too hard for scissors to cut, so stone wins over scissors; and scissors cut paper, so scissors win over paper.

The five elements were associated with the five directions, the five primary colours, and the five sacred animals. Wood, fire, metal and water were associated with Spring, Summer, Autumn and Winter (earth was excluded because it represented all of the seasons). This way of thinking led to a cosmic diagram of the world, which showed a black tortoise to the north, a green dragon to the east, a red finch to the south, a white tiger to the west, and man at the centre.

The five elements were subsequently associated with many more things, such as domestic animals, government agencies, mountains, numbers, planets, sense organs, smells, tastes, and weather. *Figure 2.*

The trigrams are eight combinations of broken and unbroken lines arranged in groups of three. They are individually named k'an, ken, chen, sun, li, k'un, tui and ch'ien. Emperor Fu Hsi (2953-2838 B.C.), who is revered as one of China's first wise men, is said to have discovered the eight trigrams by studying the markings on the shell of a tortoise. The Chinese associate the eight trigrams with everything in the universe. For example, kan is associated with ear, middle son,

ELEMENT	Wood	Fire	Earth	Metal	Water
DIRECTION	East	South	Centre	West	North
COLOUR	Blue Green	Red	Yellow	White	Black
NUMBER	8	7	5	9	6
YANG/YIN	lesser Yang	greater Yang		lesser Yin	greater Yin
SEASON	Spring	Summer		Autumn	Winter
CLIMATE	Windy	Hot	Humid	Dry	Cold
WEATHER	Wind	Heat	Sunshine	Cold	Rain
MOUNTAINS	T'ai-shan	Heng-shan (in Hunan)	Sung-shan	Hua-shan	Heng-shan (in Hopei)
PLANETS	Jupiter	Mars	Saturn	Venus	Mercury
ANIMALS	Dragon	Phoenix	Ox	Tiger	Snake Tortoise
DOMESTIC	Sheep	Fowl	Ox	Dog	Pig
CLASSES OF ANIMALS	Scaly (fishes)	Feathered (birds)	Naked (man)	Hairy (mammals)	Shell-covered (inverte-brates)
EMPERORS	Fu-Hsi	Shen-Nung	Huang-ti	Shao-hao	Chuan-hsu
THEIR ASSISTANTS	Chu Mang	Chu Jung	Hou-t'u	Ju-Shou	Hsuan-ming
ORIFICES	Eyes	Ears	Mouth	Nose	Anus Vulva
QUALITIES	Formable	Burning and ascending	Producing edible vegetation	Malleable and changeable	Soaking and descending

Figure 2

moon, north, water, Winter, and so on. The eight trigrams are combined one with another to form the sixty-four hexagrams, which are the basis of the Chinese oracle the **I Ching**. The words 'trigram' and 'hexagram' simply indicate the number of lines in each type of figure (respectively three and six).

A geomancer searches for a site where the five elements and the eight trigrams are in harmony, otherwise there will be chaos. For example, the Peak in Hong Kong is associated with wood, and a hill named Taip'ingshan - at the foot of the Peak - is associated with fire. "Now, a pile of wood with a fire at the bottom - what is the consequence?" asks Ernest J. Eitel in **Feng-shui: The Science of Sacred Landscape in Old China.** "Why, it is no wonder that most fires in Hong Kong occur in the Tai'pingshan district."[2]

Reflecting on a similar classification system from South America in **Tristes Tropiques**, Claude Levis-Strauss writes:

"We gave up sun worship a long time ago and we have lost the habit of associating the points of the compass with magic qualities, colours and virtues.... But are they really superstitions? I see these preferences rather as denoting a kind of wisdom which savage races practised spontaneously and the rejection of which, by the modern world, is the real madness.... Space has its own values, just as sounds and perfumes have colours, and feelings weight."[3]

Qi (the breath of nature) is an almighty and omnipresent energy that infuses and vitalises everything, enabling such things as mountains to form, trees to grow tall, grass to be green, flowers to bloom, and water to be fresh. The earth is criss-crossed with 'divine pipelines' that carry qi quickly from place to place. For example, Li Lung-chi, the greatest of the T'ang emperors, managed to divert qi from China's tropical provinces northwards to his park in Ch'ang-an, which caused the tangerines in the park to bear fruit unexpectedly. A geomancer indicates the spot where a house, for example, should go to take advantage of the qi flowing through the site. This is not a simple task however, because qi ebbs and flows in a sixty year cycle.[4]

"When it was proposed to construct a telegraph between Canton and Hong Kong," writes J. Dyer Ball in **Things Chinese**, "the ground of the opposition against it was as follows: Canton is the 'City of Rams', or Sheep; the mouth of the river is known as the 'Tiger's Mouth'; the District opposite Hong Kong is the 'Nine Dragons' (Kau Lung). What more unfortunate combination could be found - a telegraph line to lead the Sheep right into the Tiger's Mouth and amongst the Nine Dragons!"[5]

Telegraph lines, railway tracks, rivers, roads, walls, in fact anything straight, which geomancers call 'secret arrows', produce sha qi (noxious vapour). Sha qi travels only in a straight line, and causes bad feng-shui. A house at the end of a cul-de-sac, for example, will be hit by sha qi produced by the road. As a result, the residents of that house will suffer accidents and illnesses, and their friends will stab them in the back: like produces like. A Chinese priest or temple medium would probably blame evil spirits rather than sha qi, but the results are exactly the same.

The Chinese avoided secret arrows wherever they could. The road leading to the Ming tombs near Beijing, for example, swings east so that sha qi produced by the road will miss the tombs. But sometimes secret arrows were necessary evils. For example, a straight road made the best processional way. Even so, it at first seems strange that such an important place as the Imperial Palace in Beijing was planned along a straight axis, which is a secret arrow. However, this axis is broken at several points by moats, rivers, gateways and buildings, which block sha qi. More importantly, this axis was meant to be read as height, not length. "No matter how the natural terrain of China is formed," writes Nelson Wu in **Chinese & Indian Architecture**, "one always goes *up* to Peking."[6] *Figure 3.*

The two classical schools of feng-shui

There are two common methods of practising feng-shui. One involves searching the landscape for symbolic forms, which is called the 'Form school'. For example, in **The Chinese Looking Glass** Dennis Bloodworth writes:

"Where the railway crosses the border between the Chinese provinces of Kwangtung and Hunan, there is a curious mountain upon whose

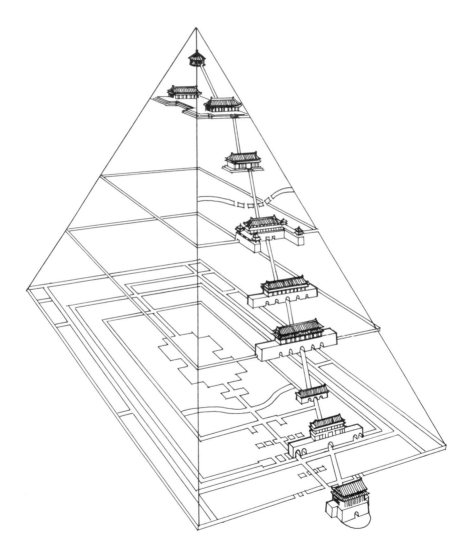

Figure 3

summit stands a rock as big as a house but shaped like a chicken. This zoomorphic slab of stone has naturally excited the Kwangtung geomancers, who have long predicted that the spirit of the Golden Chicken would take the form of a Kwangtung hero. In due course, local boy indeed made good, for a man called Hsueh Yueh, born in the very country within which Golden Chicken Mountain stands, became one of China's most able generals. The geomancers were further vindicated when he was appointed regional commander of the military zone that included Hunan Province, for the stone chicken had its beak pointing into Hunan, but its bottom in Kwangtung. It therefore fed on Hunan but laid its golden eggs in Kwangtung, and a Kwangtung general with power over Hunan would presumably do the same thing: the people of Hunan were going to end up the poorer, and those of Kwangtung very much richer. The stubborn and pugnacious inhabitants of Hunan…were furious that this foreigner should be appointed over them, expected the worst, and proceeded to remedy the situation by climbing the Golden Chicken and breaking off its offending beak."[7]

This story also illustrates the Chinese belief that luck is finite, and one person's good fortune equals another person's misfortune: before the chicken's beak was broken off, the people of Kwangtung were lucky *because* the people of Hunan were unlucky.

A lucky site reflects the cosmic diagram of the world that I described earlier. The black tortoise takes the form of a high mountain to the north, the green dragon a slightly lower mountain to the east, the white tiger an even lower mountain to the west, and the red finch a meandering river to the south. *Figure 4.* The Ming tombs near Beijing are on such a site. Where the land is flat, however, the black tortoise may take the form of a lake, the green dragon a grove of trees, the white tiger a road, and the red finch an open plain.

The 'Compass School' is the other common method of practising feng-shui. It involves the use of a luopan, which consists of a compass set in the middle of a circular wooden board inscribed with eight or more rings of esoteric letters and symbols that represent a host of concepts, including the eight trigrams, the five elements, and yang and yin. *Figure 5.* A geomancer discovers whether a certain place is lucky by interpreting the letters and symbols indicated by the needle of the compass. In fact

Figure 4

the Chinese used compasses for feng-shui before they used them for navigation. A luopan is also a powerful talisman: in Singapore I saw one propped up on a shelf in the corner of a restaurant to turn back sha qi.

But sometimes the method of divination is unconventional. For example, a geomancer in Berkeley, California reviewed three sites for a peace park near Lincoln, Nebraska, by simply moving his hands over a map of Lincoln. The site he favoured had two major high-

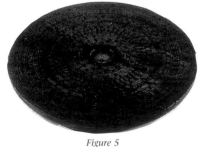

Figure 5

ways to the north, a Methodist college to the east, a Catholic retreat to the south, and a medical laboratory to the west. He predicted that the traffic on the highways, the religious centres, and the medical laboratory would all generate a lot of good energy for the peace park.

An even more unconventional method of divination is described by Wu Ching-Tzu in **The Scholars**. Two geomancers are asked to determine the feng-shui of a grave from some clods of soil. After examining the soil very carefully, they eat some of it. "This soil is no good!" one geomancer announces. "If you bury someone in this, you will bankrupt your family," explains the other.[8]

Ways of improving bad feng-shui

It is first come first served, so the number of sites with good feng-shui usually declines as more people move into an area. But a geomancer can improve the feng-shui of a site by constructing earthworks, pagodas or walls in certain places.

"On the northern side of the palace, at the distance of a bow-shot but still within the walls, the Great Khan has had made an earthwork, that is to say a mound fully 100 paces in height and over a mile in circumference," writes Marco Polo in **The Travels**.[9] This man-made hill, which corresponded with the cosmic diagram's black tortoise, would have improved the feng-shui of Kublai Khan's palace.

In exactly the same way, Jing-shan (Coal Hill), which is also man-made, improves the feng-shui of the Forbidden City. When Jing-shan is seen from the air it resembles a man sitting in meditation: the halls at the foot of the hill form his head, the cypress trees his beard, and the hill his body. *Figure 6*. This auspicious symbolism also enhances the feng-shui of the Forbidden City.

The town of Tsuen-cheu-fu, which was shaped in plan like a carp, was frequently plundered by the inhabitants of neighbouring Yung-chun, which was shaped in plan like a fishing net, until two tall pagodas were built in Tsuen-cheu-fu to intercept the imaginary fishing net of Yung-chun. This shows that tall stuctures may or may not improve feng-shui,

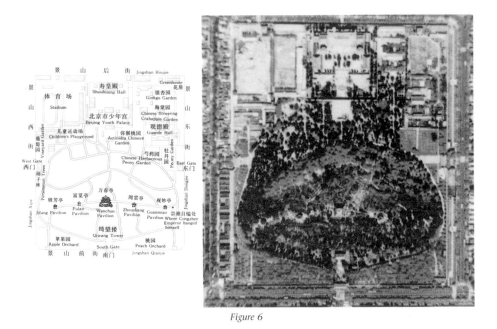

Figure 6

depending upon your point of view: the pagodas improved the feng-shui of Tsuen-cheu-fu, but spoiled the feng-shui of Yung-chun.

In China, many houses have a cross wall built a little distance from the front door, either inside or outside or both, as a barrier to sha qi. *Figures 7-9*. These walls, which are called 'ying-pei' (spirit screens), · are probably the best known manifestations of feng-shui in the West. I have even found descriptions of them in three mystery stories by American authors: **The Chinese Orange Mystery** by Ellery Queen, **Thank You Mr. Moto** by John P. Marquand, and **The Flying Chinaman** by Harry H. Fein.[10]

Skewing a door away from an offending secret arrow is a more elegant solution than a wall. I have seen this done to doors in many houses in Anhui province in China, the Bright Hill temple in Singapore, and one restaurant in

Figure 7

Figures 8–9

Figure 10

Figure 11

Figure 12

Figure 13

Figure 14

Figure 15

Little Bourke Street, the heart of Melbourne's Chinatown. *Figures 10-15*. This solution requires forethought, however, because it may be quite difficult to accomplish once a building has been completed.

Mirrors and charms are the simplest forms of protection against sha qi. *Figure 16*. I have a mirror hanging above my front door at home, which turns back sha qi produced by the roof ridge of the house opposite. When someone asks me 'Has the mirror made you lucky?' I answer 'No, but who knows how many disasters it has averted!'

Figure 16

Mirrors are used to overcome so many causes of bad feng-shui that Sarah Rossbach describes them as "the aspirin of feng-shui" in her book **Feng-shui: The Chinese Art of Placement**.[11]

A ba-gua (eight sided diagram) is another very effective cure-all for bad feng-shui. It usually consists of an octagonal piece of wood, inscribed with the eight trigrams around the yang and yin symbol. *Figure 17*. Several shops in Little Bourke Street have a ba-gua hanging above the

Figure 17

Figure 18   *Figure 19*

front door, or painted on the front window, which protects the shops from sha qi. Sometimes in the latter cases, at first glance the ba-gua appears to have been painted on the window just for decoration, but in fact it is 'functional'. *Figures 18 & 19.*

Chinese priests or temple mediums issue charms against evil spirits which are usually written on strips of paper, cloth or wood, and placed above doors and windows. *Figure 20.* Typically, one might read:

"The god of thunder hereby orders the four genii who preside officially over the year to proceed on a tour of inspection and seize all discontented orbate ghosts. Moreover, the god of heaven is commanded to repress the malevolent stellar gods who disturb the peace and happiness of mortals."[12]

Good luck may be enhanced by decorating a house with auspicious symbols. Take for example just the front door of a house I saw near Suzhou in China. The handle was a replica of an ancient Chinese coin (symbol of wealth and prosperity), the bolt was topped with two peaches (symbol of longevity), and the escutcheon was shaped like a bat (symbol of happiness). *Figures 21-23.*

Feng-shui in Kuching, Malaysia

On a trip to Kuching in East Malaysia in 1985 I observed how some Chinese shopkeepers remedied bad feng-shui caused by tall buildings, and also how they protected their doors and windows from sha qi.

Three brothers ran a shop in Courthouse Road, directly opposite the courthouse. Business was bad and the brothers were quarrelling, so they consulted a Chinese temple medium to find out what was wrong. The temple medium blamed the brothers' troubles on the courthouse: it was much taller than the brothers' shop, and it drew qi away from the shop because it was such an important building. The temple medium told the brothers to fix a Chinese paintbrush, a circle of rattan, a dried plant, a white electric light, and a swastika above a first floor window of the shop. *Figure 24.*

Figure 20

Also, to burn joss sticks in front of the shop during the day, and switch on the white electric light at night. The brothers did exactly what the temple medium suggested and business improved and they stopped quarrelling.

A woman living in a shop in India Street became mysteriously ill, so her children consulted a Chinese temple medium to find out what had caused her illness. The temple medium blamed the woman's illness on the building across the street, which was one and a half storeys taller than the woman's shop. The temple medium advised the woman's children to hang a mirror and a pair of scissors above a first floor window of the shop. *Figure 25.* The children followed the temple

Figure 21   *Figures 22–23*

Figures 24

medium's instructions and their mother got better. When the occupant of the building across the street saw the mirror and the scissors he hung a ba-gua and a fan above a second floor window of his shop to try to win back his feng-shui advantage. This illustrates how feng-shui quarrels start. In **The Religious Systems of China** J.J.M. DeGroot writes:

"Quarrels and litigation arising from changes are a daily occurrence in Chinese towns. The repairing of a house, the building of a wall or dwelling, especially if it overtops its surroundings, the planting of a pole or the cutting down of a tree, in short any change in our ordinary position of objects, may disturb the good luck of the house and temples in the vicinity, and of the whole quarter, and cause the people to be visited by disasters, misery and death."[13]

A shop in Khoo Hun Yeang Street had a sword in a clay pot and a fan above a first floor window, which protected the shop from sha qi produced by buses leaving the bus station across the street. *Figure 26*. The shop next door had a fan, a ba-gua and a mirror above a first floor window for the same reason. *Figure 27*. Apparently these charms were unsuccessful because both shops had gone out of business.

At a T-junction in Carpenter Street stood a shop with a ba-gua, a fan and a mirror above the front door, which protected the shop from sha qi produced by the straight road. The shopkeeper said these charms also stopped qi flowing out of the shop.

Another shop in Main Bazaar had a ba-gua, a mirror and a pair of scissors above the front door to protect the place from sha qi produced by a straight corridor in the warehouse across the street, and also to stop qi flowing out. *Figure 28*. The shop was not at risk when the doors of the warehouse were closed, however.

Both in Kuching and Singapore I have seen cacti in pots used as a protection against sha qi. *Figure 29*.

How can seemingly mundane objects, such as mirrors, fans, swords and scissors turn back sha qi? A fan blows sha qi away, a mirror reflects sha qi back to where it came from (also, evil spirits take off in fright when they see themselves reflected in a mirror), and swords and scissors look threatening (also, evil spirits are weakened by iron objects). However,

Figures 25–28

the shopkeepers in Kuching could not tell me how these objects also stopped qi from flowing away and overcame bad feng-shui caused by tall buildings. The fact that these objects are powerful Taoist symbols may be the answer. A pair of scissors, a ruler, a mirror and a sword were offered to the gods during the ceremonial opening of a new Chinese temple at Kandang, Malacca, in December 1938. S.M. Middlebrook explains:

Figure 29

"These represent the guiding principles of the Taoist faith. With the scissors you 'cut your coat according to the cloth you have': with the ruler you 'measure the standards necessary to life and live accordingly': with the mirror 'you let your actions and your conscience be as clear as the glass into which you look': and with the sword 'you cut down that which is bad and face the world with principles as shining as the blade.'"[14]

The Chinese shopkeepers I interviewed in Kuching all thought that good feng-shui was important because it meant good business. Nevertheless, they somehow reminded me of Mr. Irquetson's friend in **Conrad in Quest of His Youth** by Leonard Merrick. Mr. Irquetson says to Conrad:

"Once...I was passing with a friend through Grosvenor Street. ...and we came to a ladder leaning against a house that was being redecorated. In stepping to the other side of the ladder, my friend lifted his hat to it; you may know the superstition? ...I said, 'Is it possible that you believe in that nonsense?' He said, 'N-no, I don't exactly believe in it, but I never throw away a chance.'"[15]

Feng-shui in Victoria, Australia during the goldrush

Feng-shui influenced the siting, design and decoration of the Chinese joss house in Bendigo - one of only a handful of Chinese structures left in Victoria that were built during the goldrush. ('Joss' may be a corruption of 'deos', which was used by sixteenth century Portuguese mariners to describe the gods and idols worshipped in the East Indies.) Like everyone else on the goldfields, the Chinese needed plenty of good luck, so naturally they continued to practise feng-shui in Australia. Many Chinese miners owned a copy of the ancient Chinese almanack called the **Tong Shu**, which contained information on such things as charms, feng-shui, fortune-telling, herbal medicine, and lucky and unlucky days. Jean Gittins in **The Diggers from China** writes:

"Even though the seasons in the strange land were reputed to be topsyturvy, it was hoped that life would continue to be guided not only by seasonal variations recorded in the almanac, but by advice set down for matters of daily routine. It would, for example, be advantageous to know the exact day on which proposed ventures gave promise of successful conclusion or when it would be wiser to step quietly to avoid meeting up with evil spirits."[16]

The Bendigo joss house consists of three separate buildings - a caretaker's residence, a temple dedicated to Quan Gong, and an ancestral hall. *Figures 30-33*. The joss house is situated on high ground, between two creeks, which should make the local community lucky, wealthy and prosperous. There should be good harvests in the area because there is alluvial soil north and south of the joss house. The site of the joss house is a triangle, which is often associated with outbreaks of fire and other calamities. However, these problems are avoided here because the main entrances do not face a Y-junction. The joss house is set back a long way from the main road, to protect it from noise and pollution, and the road is on the south side of the temple, which is desirable from a feng-shui point of view. There is a fish-pond directly in front of the temple, and a creek and a lake to the south-east of the site, which are sources of qi. There are no trees or buildings in front of the joss house because they may harbour evil spirits, and obstruct the flow of qi.

The internal dimensions of the joss house are lucky.* The joss house faces south because qi emanates from there. No doors or windows face

---

* A geomancer's ruler is divided into eight parts. Dimensions that fall within the first, fourth, fifth and eighth parts of the ruler are considered to be lucky.

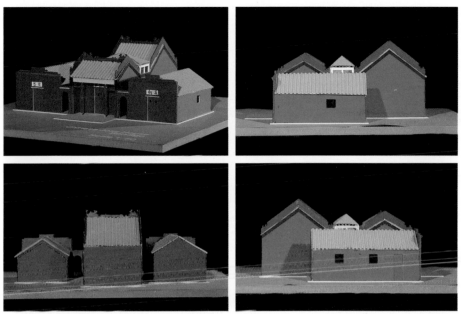

Figures 30–33

north because sha qi emanates from there. The thresholds are raised, to prevent sha qi passing under the doors. The path between the three buildings is staggered, to deny sha qi a direct route through the joss house. The joss house is painted in auspicious colours - the walls, the columns and the doors are red, the bases of the columns are green, and the gables of the temple are black and yellow. Each colour is associated with yang or yin, an element, a trigram, and so on.

The temple is located centrally because it is more important than the other buildings, which is desirable from a feng-shui point of view. It is also grander than the other buildings. For example, the front wall is adorned with auspicious symbols; a pair of stone lions, which symbolise yang and yin, guard the front doors; and stylised dancing dragons, which symbolise power and authority, decorate the ends of the ridges.

The South Melbourne joss house, which is bigger and grander than the one at Bendigo, was also sited, designed and decorated according to feng-shui principles. For example, the joss house faces southeast, and no doors or windows face northwest. *Figures 34 & 35*. However, when the joss house was built in the 1860's, no one considered the possible

Figures 34–35

development of the surrounding land in the future, and subsequently the good feng-shui of the site of the joss house was ruined. When it opened in 1866, it was the only building in the vicinity; it stood on a slight hill, overlooking South Park Lagoon (now Albert Park Lake) and Port Phillip Bay; and the nearest main road, Clarendon Street (the white tiger), was west of the joss house, which was desirable from a feng-shui point of view. However, the slight hill 'disappeared' when the surrounding land was levelled for subdivision in the early 1900's, and the views of South Park Lagoon and Port Phillip Bay were soon blocked by new buildings. The construction of new roads also caused problems. According to one feng-shui rule of thumb, the construction of Cobden and Raglan Streets, north and south of the joss house, made it easier to burgle the joss house. Also, the construction of Raglan Place created a secret arrow aimed at the joss house.

It appears that the siting of the Chinese goldminers' graves in some Victorian cemeteries was influenced by feng-shui. Take for example the Chinese sections of the Maldon and Campbell's Creek cemeteries. They may not be model feng- shui sites, but they were the best the Chinese could do within the confines of European-style cemeteries.

At Maldon the Chinese graves are situated on a gentle, south-sloping hill. "Chinese Ground" is written in both Chinese and English characters on the largest of the headstones. The headstones were erected at auspicious times, which is stated on them in Chinese. At the bottom of the hill is a very fine, red-brick, hexagonal-shaped burning tower, which is crowned with a cement rendered gourd, the symbol of Li T'ieh-kuai, the most famous of the Eight Immortals, and the source of magic spells. *Figure 36.* Beyond the burning tower is a gently flowing creek. A large hill to the northeast of the cemetry 'protects' the Chinese graves.

At Campbell's Creek the Chinese graves and a burning tower are also situated on a gentle south-sloping hill. *Figure 37.* At the foot of the hill is a seasonal creek. The European graves, on the other hand, are on a flat plain, facing east.

Some Western encounters with feng-shui

China fascinated many English artists, craftsmen and architects during the eighteenth century, which greatly influenced their work. Sir

Figure 36

Figure 37

William Chambers' redesign of Kew gardens (c. 1757), for example, imitated the spontaneous irregularity and asymmetrical planning of many Chinese gardens, qualities that Sir William Temple had earlier described as 'sharawadgi'. The origin of the word is a puzzle, but I suspect it may have been a gross corruption of 'feng-shui', which is certainly what Temple meant by it:

"Something of this I have seen in some places, but heard more of it from others, who have lived much among the *Chineses*, a People whose way of thinking seems to lie as wide of ours in *Europe,* as their Country does.... Their greatest reach of Imagination is employed in contriving Figures, where the Beauty shall be great and strike the Eye, but without any order or disposition of parts, that shall be commonly or easily observ'd. And though we have hardly any Notion of this sort of Beauty, yet they have a particular Word to express it, and where they find it hit their Eye at first sight, they say the *Sharawadgi* is fine or is admirable, or any such expression of Esteem...."[17]

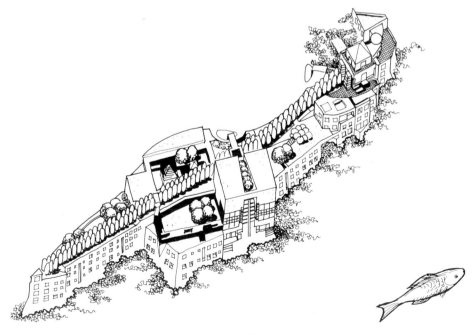

Figure 38

More recently, some Western architects who have designed buildings in Hong Kong have had to take feng-shui into consideration. For example, PDCM, a firm of architects from Melbourne, designed a luxury residential club in Hong Kong, which had good feng-shui. In feng-shui terms, the site of the club was shaped like a leaping fish. PDCM placed a penthouse and four luxury apartments on the fish's head, the club's facilities and twenty appartments on the fish's body, and fifteen studios on the fish's tail. *Figure 38.* This design won second prize in the Peak competition, which was held in 1983. Curiously, the winning entry made no specific references to feng-shui.

British architect Norman Foster consulted a geomancer when he was designing the Hong Kong and Shanghai Bank building in Hong Kong. The geomancer suggested where to put the main entrance to the building - not directly at the front, but angled to one side. He also placed the escalators that lead from the public plaza to the main banking floor at odd angles. *Figure 39.* Later he arranged the furniture in the senior

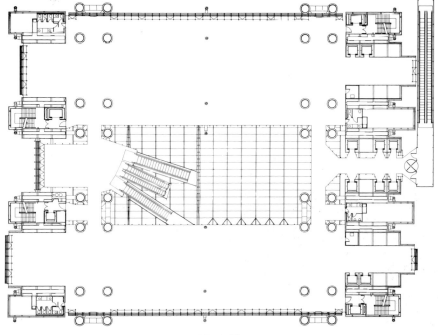

Figure 39

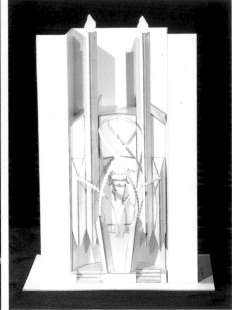

Figures 40–42

executives' offices, and supervised the relocation of a pair of bronze lions from outside the old building to outside the new one.

In 1988 I asked a group of architecture students from the Royal Melbourne Institute of Technology to design a small town house for a Chinese couple, which was deliberately located at a T-junction in "Bad Luck Street". The fabric of the building had to turn away sha qi instead of relying on charms above doors and windows, which were usually afterthoughts. The students experimented with armour plating, gargoyles, jagged edges, mirrored glass, obscured doorways, pools of water, sharp sticks, small windows, screen walls and twisted metal. Some of these things would have also helped to over-come some of the mundane problems associated with living in a house facing oncoming traffic, such as excessive noise. The students' designs would have made interesting buildings regardless of whether you believed in feng-shui or not. *Figures 40-42.*

As I stated earlier, feng-shui is mentioned in several mystery stories by American authors. For example, in *The Spy and the Geomancers* by Edward D. Hoch, British Intelligence employs a geomancer named Leslie Wo to predict where the government of the People's Republic of China will build in Hong Kong and the New Territories. As Wo explains:

"...Hong Kong is scheduled to be returned to the People's Republic of China on July 1, 1997, when the British mandate expires. ...the Chinese...will seek the advice of geomancers on the most favourable sites for new construction.... Wouldn't British Intelligence be interested in knowing, several years in advance, exactly where on this island and in the New Territories the Chinese will be building? Every airbase, every missile launcher, every radar station? The entire defense posture of Hong Kong as it will be in ten or twenty years?"[18]

Furniture arrangement

In 1978 Dean Wakefield, an executive with Dow Chemical, employed a geomancer to rearrange the furniture in his office in Hong Kong after he and his staff had a run of bad luck: Wakefield returned from an unsuccessful business trip to find that his secretary, who was in the early stages of pregnancy, was off work with severe abdominal pains; his assistant had just learned that his baby son needed serious eye surgery; and another assistant's wife had just suffered her third miscarriage. Wakefield knew an American freelance journalist who had employed a geomancer to look at her flat in Hong Kong after she had had a run of bad luck. The day after she followed the geomancer's advice she unexpectedly received payment for two of her magazine articles.

Wakefield suggested to his staff that they should also seek advice from a geomancer.

Wakefield employed the geomancer who had advised his friend. The geomancer spoke no English so Wakefield asked his Chinese staff to take notes, which they carefully compared after the geomancer had left. Also, Wakefield did not want to rely on what just one of them said because they had all heard feng-shui recommendations before and considered themselves at least minor experts on the subject.

The geomancer said that evil spirits swooped down steeply sloping Garden Road and entered their office building. The arrow-like symbol on the Cable and Wireless building, which they could see from their office, pointed straight at them and showed the evil spirits where to go. The geomancer said they should always keep their blinds closed.

He also advised them to rearrange their desks to face southwest. Facing south was second best. Two of them had been facing north, which was very unlucky. The geomancer told them to move their desks on either one of two auspicious dates that he provided.

The two secretaries had to put a yellow ceramic cow on their desk. The others had to put a black ceramic fish on the window sill in their office. They also had to put a bamboo plant in the southeast corner of their office.

Finally, the geomancer predicted that 60 days after they had moved their desks, they would experience very good luck. He was paid about forty dollars for his advice. I shall let Dean Wakefield finish the story:

"We all went to the race track on the 60th day after the office rearrangement. I lost about one hundred and forty dollars. I had to dismiss my secretary because she did not return from her holidays when she said she would. I heard she later had a miscarriage. My assistant's baby son did not need to have corrective eye surgery - eyeglasses did the job after all. After having three miscarriages, my assistant's wife gave birth to a girl. They are now divorced. I came back to the United States in 1980 and also got divorced. If I had the chance I'd do the whole over in a trice!"[19]

Malay-style feng-shui

Systems of divination similar in character to feng-shui exist in many cultures. The first step in the Malay building process, for example, is finding a suitable site. There are so many variables to consider, however, that usually a pawang (a shaman who specialises in building matters) is consulted.

Land that faces a river or a valley is considered best for the site of a house. Land that rises to the west brings good luck, respectability and wealth. Land that rises to the north brings happiness and good health. White soil that smells fragrant and tastes sweet brings affluence, respectability, and protection from evil. Also, one member of the family will become a religious expert. Yellow soil that smells fragrant brings good luck and enormous wealth. Red soil that tastes sour brings peace and religion. Yellowish, reddish or greenish soil brings good luck in business, and good health. Also, the family will not have nightmares. Coarse soil that tastes hot and sweet, increases fertility.

On the other hand, a hillside is unsuitable for the site of a house because evil spirits live there. Swampy land is to be avoided because it is the home of evil genies and ghosts that cause sickness. Similarly, land full of holes is bad because living there are supernatural creatures that destroy good luck and cause nightmares and strange sicknesses. The site of an abandoned well should not be used because evil spirits that throw stones and sand may have made it their home. Also, abandoned wells are sometimes used in tests of physical and mental strength, and often old charms to cure the sick are thrown down them. Land that rises to the south brings bad luck and poverty; land that rises to the east brings hardship and sudden death; and finally, black soil that smells foul is unsuitable for house building.

Once a promising site has been found the pawang will seek an omen. For example, he may leave a bottle of water on the site overnight. If the water level has increased by next morning the site is good. If it has decreased, however, the site is bad. If all is well the pawang will choose an auspicious time to start work on the house. In general, the best month for building a house is Ramaddhan (the ninth month of the

Muslim year), and the best days for working on a house are Thursdays, Fridays and Saturdays.

To ensure that a person will have good luck and great wealth, the front door of his house should face either north or west. To deny evil spirits a direct route through a house and to prevent male visitors from seeing into the women's part of a house, the front door must never be in line with any other doors of the house.

Western-style feng-shui

During the nineteenth century, many Chinese in Hong Kong believed that the English were feng-shui experts because they chanced to settle in places which had excellent feng-shui. This probably amused the English colonists, since most of them dismissed feng-shui as mumbo jumbo. However, systems of divination similar in character to feng-shui once also existed in the West. The Roman architect Vitruvius, who lived in the first century B.C., describes a Roman system of divination in **The Ten Books on Architecture**. For example, he says:

"First comes the choice of a very healthy site [for a town]. Such a site will be high, neither misty nor frosty, and in a climate neither hot nor cold, but temperate: further, without marshes in the neighbourhood. For when the morning breezes blow toward the town at sunrise, if they bring with them mists from marshes and, mingled with the mist, the poisonous breath of the creatures of the marshes to be wafted into the bodies of the inhabitants, they will make the site unhealthy."[20]

I think that a Chinese geomancer would agree with Vitruvius, although he would probably say 'a site with good feng-shui' instead of "a very healthy site", and 'sha qi' instead of "the poisonous breath of the creatures of the marshes". Vitruvius also describes how wind and water affected the health of the inhabitants of certain towns, which is interesting, remembering that 'feng-shui' is Chinese for 'wind and water'. For example, he says:

"Mytilene in the island of Lesbos is a town built with magnificence and good taste, but its position shows a lack of foresight. In that community when the wind is south, the people fall ill; when it is northwest, it sets them coughing; with a north wind they do indeed recover but cannot stand about in the alleys and streets, owing to the severe cold."[21]

A Chinese geomancer would probably say that Mytilene had bad feng-shui, and suggest some way of remedying it, like planting groves of trees at certain places to act as windbreaks. Wind was synonymous with evil in China, thus it was avoided in many traditional structures, regardless of the benefits of ventilation.

A colourful description of an English system of divination may be found in Ben Jonson's play **The Alchemist**, which was first performed in 1610 in Oxford. Abel Drugger, a tobacco-man, asks Subtle, the alchemist, how to set up his new shop:

> "I am a young beginner and am building
> Of a new shop, an't like your worship, just
> At corner of a street. Here's the plot on't.
> And I would know, by art, sir, of your worship,
> Which way I should make my door, by necromancy,
> And where my shelves, and which should be for boxes,
> And which for pots. I would be glad to thrive, sir.
> And I was wished to your worship by a gentleman,
> One Captain Face, that says you know men's planets,
> And their good angels and their bad."[22]

Subtle furnishes the advice he is asked for. He says:

> "Make me your door, then, south; your broad side, west;
> And on the east side of your shop, aloft,
> Write 'Mathlai', 'Tarmiel' and 'Baraborat';
> Upon the north part, 'Rael', 'Velel', 'Thiel'.
> They are the names of those Mercurial spirits
> That do fright flies from boxes.... And,
> Beneath your threshold, bury me a loadstone
> To draw in gallants that wear spurs. The rest
> They'll seem to follow....
> And, on your stall, a puppet, with a vice,
> And a court-fucus, to call city-dames.
> You shall deal much with minerals."[23]

Drugger also asks Subtle:

> "...to look over...my almanack,
> And cross out my ill-days that I may neither
> Bargain nor trust upon them."[24]

Subtle's style of necromancy - to use Drugger's term - appears to have much in common with feng-shui, but as far as I know, the two are not linked historically. Subtle advises Drugger on astrology, charms, orientation, planning and spirits, just as a geomancer might advise a Chinese shopkeeper. Also, Drugger seeks Subtle's advice so his business may thrive, which is why many Chinese shopkeepers seek feng-shui advice.

Subtle tells Drugger to bury a loadstone, which is a magnetised piece of iron ore, under the threshold of his shop, to attract customers wearing spurs. But a loadstone would have also repelled fairies, witches and demons from Drugger's shop, because they were disempowered by iron. Similarly, a horseshoe attracted good luck on the one hand, because it was crescent-shaped, like the symbol of the moon goddess, and repelled evil spirits on the other, because they were weakened by the iron of the horseshoe. In **Master Humphrey's Clock** Charles Dickens describes how horseshoes were used as charms in Windsor during the reign of King James the First:

"The inhabitants boiled a witch on the king's birthday and sent a bottle of the broth to court, with dutiful address expressive of their loyalty. The king, being rather frightened by the present, piously bestowed it upon the Archbishop of Canterbury, and returned an answer to the address, wherein he gave them golden rules for discovering witches, and laid great stress upon certain protecting charms, and especially horseshoes. Immediately the towns-people went to work nailing up horseshoes over every door, and so many anxious parents apprenticed their children to farriers to keep them out of harm's way, that it became quite a genteel trade, and flourished exceedingly."[25]

To return to **The Alchemist**, Drugger asks Subtle to look at his 'almanack' and cross out his unlucky days. During Elizabethan, Stuart and early Georgian times, an almanack was the Western counterpart of the **Tong Shu**. It was a calendar of the days of the year, which noted such things as the phases of the moon, saints' days, seasonal festivals, and the times of sunrise and sunset. It also contained information on such things as astrology, farming, folklore, fortune-telling and meteorology, which was often reduced to a rhyme or a rule-of-thumb, so it might be remembered easily. For example, it is unlucky to take anything out of the house on New Year's day, but if you must, be sure to bring something inside first. This is stated as a rhyme in **The Perpetual Almanack of Folklore**:

> *Take out, then take in,*
> *Bad luck will begin;*
> *Take in, then take out,*
> *Good luck comes about.* [26]

Some almanacks are still published, such as **Old Moore's Almanack**, but they are merely novel anachronisms without any real authority. Nowadays home improvement magazines have replaced almanacks as the main source of collected wisdom on such topics as house design, furniture layout, colour schemes, and gardening. For example, I believe that many houses and gardens look 'right' from one viewpoint only because the occupants of those houses have copied an illustration in a home improvement magazine which was photographed or drawn from one carefully chosen viewpoint.

In **Common Landscape of America, 1580 to 1845**, John Stilgoe writes:

"Even as late as the nineteenth century, settlers in the Ohio Valley sited farmhouses 'right with the earth,' parallel to vaguely understood lines of force that directed good health and prosperity to well-placed doors."[27]

Many people also believed that the magnetic forces of the earth influenced their well-being. Alignment with these forces was reputed to be healthful, and nonalignment harmful. Charles Dickens, for example, oriented his bed on a north-south axis with the headboard towards north, believing that it promoted restful sleep and good health. These ideas were very similar to feng-shui and qi. But, ironically, about the same time as they were current in America and England, English colonists and missionaries were deriding the Chinese for believing in feng-shui. For example, in **Things Chinese** J. Dyer Ball dismisses feng-shui as a "farrago of nonsense";[28] while in **A Winter in China** Reverend T.M. Morris writes:

"The dark thread of this superstition is woven warp and woof into the very fabric of Chinese life...There is nothing too marvellous for a Chinaman to believe; and nearly every Chinaman is the victim, to an extent that is to us almost incredible, of superstitious and childish fears."[29]

Although Western-style feng-shui is now extinct, a few closely related ideas have survived. For example, in several Western countries horseshoes are sometimes still hung above doors for good luck, and some people living in Melbourne appear to have turned their letterboxes into protective charms. Every home in Australia must have a letterbox for the delivery of mail, which is nearly always located on the street boundary for the convenience of the postman. While a fence is usually enough to reinforce this boundary and physically protect a home from intruders, I have seen letterboxes which look like heavy artillery that may spiritually protect those homes from thieves. *Figures 43-45*. I have also seen letterboxes made from disused fire alarms, fire extinguishers and fire hydrants that may spiritually protect those homes from fire. *Figures 46-48*. However, one thing is certain - they are not *just* letterboxes.

The expression "coming from the wrong side of the tracks" and buildings without a thirteenth floor show that we still consider some places to be unlucky. The Chinese author Chiang Yee thought the former custom was very odd, just as many Western authors thought that feng-shui was very strange. In **The Silent Traveller in New York**, he writes:

"I had heard that most downtown skyscrapers have no thirteenth floor, the number of storeys being therefore one less than that claimed. Everyone in this part of the city, it was said, dreads bad luck and will have nothing to do with thirteen. How, I wondered, do they count their money when it adds up to thirteen dollars? Leave one out?"[30]

Conclusion

In the West, the role of the geomancer was gradually demystified, watered down, and split up among architects, builders, conservation-

Figures 43–48

ists, environmentalists, geographers, geologists, interior designers, landscape architects, planners, real estate agents, surveyors, and numerous government agencies. I believe we are the poorer for this today because the whole was much more than the sum of its parts.

In my opinion, Western-style feng-shui was superseded by a system of building ceremonies related to turning the first sod, laying the foundation-stone, completing the roof framing, and opening the new building. Even though this system of building ceremonies is as ancient as Western-style feng-shui, if not older, I believe some current practices represent the new order which Louis Aragon elegantly describes in **Paris Peasant:**

"Man no longer worships the gods on their heights. Solomon's temple has slid into a world of metaphor where it harbours swallows' nests and corpse-white lizards. The spirit of religions, coming down to dwell in the dust, has abandoned the sacred places. But there are other places which flourish among mankind, places where men go calmly about their mysterious lives and in which a profound religion is very gradually taking shape. These sites are not yet inhabited by a divinity. It is forming there, a new godhead precipitating in these re-creations of Ephesus like acid-gnawed metal at the bottom of a glass."[31]

Notes

1. Morris, Rev. T.M. (1892), **A Winter in North China**, Fleming H. Revell Company, New York, p.229.

2. Eitel, E.J. (1873), **Feng-shui: The Science of Sacred Landscape in Old China**, Graham Brash, Singapore, 1985, p.47.

3. Levi-Strauss, C. (1955), **Tristes Tropiques**, Penguin Books Ltd., Harmondsworth, 1978. [Translated by J. and D. Weightman.] p.153-154.

4 The Ten Heavenly stems, named jia, yi, bing, ding, wu, ji, geng, xin, ren and gui, are frequently used to denote numerical order. The Twelve Earthly Branches, named zi, chou, yin, mao, chen, si, wu, wei, shen, you, xu and hai, were used in ancient times to record chronological order. The Chinese denote each year with one of the Ten Heavenly Stems and one of the Twelve Earthly Branches. For example, the Revolution of 1911 is known as the 'xin hai' Revolution in all Chinese writings. Coupling the Stems and the Branches in a regular sequence like this produces sixty pairs of characters, or a sixty year cycle.

5. Ball, J.D. (1903), **Things Chinese**, Graham Brash, 1989, p.266.

6. Wu, N.I. (1963), **Chinese & Indian Architecture**, Studio Vista Limited, London, 1968, p.43.

7. Bloodworth, D. (1966), **The Chinese Looking Glass**, Farrar Straus Giroux, New York, 1980, p.244.

8. Wu C.T., **The Scholars**, Foreign Languages Press, Peking, 1983. [Translated by Yang Hsien-Yi and G. Yang.] p. 500.

9. Polo, M., **The Travels**, Penguin Books Ltd., Harmondsworth, 1978. [Translated by R. Latham.] p.27.

10. Queen, E. (1934), **The Chinese Orange Mystery**, Penguin Books Ltd., Harmondsworth, 1956, p.102; Marquand, J. P. (1936), **Thank You Mr. Moto**, Bestseller Library, number 12, New York, p.52; and Fein, H.H. (1938), **The Flying Chinaman**, Alfred A. Knopf, New York, p.5.

11. Rossbach, S. (1983), **Feng-shui: The Chinese Art of Placement**, E.P. Dutton Inc., New York, p.68.

12. Dore, H. (1914-1929), **Researches into Chinese Superstitions**, volume IV, T'usewei Printing Press, Shanghai. [Translated by M. Kennelly.] p.317.

13. DeGroot, J.J.M. (1897), **The Religious System of China**, vol.3, Brill, Leiden, p.1041.

14. Middlebrook, S.M., *Ceremonial Opening of a New Chinese Temple at Kandang, Malacca, in December, 1938*, Journal Malayan Branch Royal Asiatic Society, vol.XVII, part I, 1939, p.105.

15. Merrick, L. **Conrad in Quest of his Youth**, Hodder & Stoughton, London. [Introduction by J.M. Barrie] p.75.

16. Gittins, J. (1981), **The Diggers from China**, Quartet Books, Melbourne, p.28.

17. Lang, S., and Pevsner, N., *Sir William Temple and Sharawaggi*, Architectural Review, 16, 1949, pp.391-393.

18. Hoch, E.D. (1989), *The Spy and the Geomancers, Ellery Queen's mystery magazine*, October 1989, p.67.

19. A letter from Dean Wakefield to Derham Groves, 1984.

20. Vitruvius, **The Ten Books on Architecture**, Dover Publications Inc., New York, 1960. [Translated by M.H. Morgan.] p.17.

21. ibid., p.25.

22. Jonson, B. **The Alchemist**, Cambridge University Press, Cambridge, 1967. [Edited by J.B. Steane.] p.46.

23. ibid., pp.48-49.

24. ibid., p.50.

25. Dickens, C. (1870), **Edwin Drood & Master Humphrey's Clock**, Chapman & Hall Ltd., Covent Garden, 1907, pp.311-312.

26. Kightly, C. (1987), **The Perpetual Almanac of Folklore**, Thames and Hudson, London, unpaged.

27. Stilgoe, J. (1982), **Common Landscape of America, 1580 to 1845**, Yale University Press, New Haven, p. 149.

28. Ball, p.265.

29. Morris, p.229 & 233.

30. Yee, C. (1950), **The Silent Traveller in New York**, Methuen & Co. Ltd., London, p.135.

31. Aragon, L. (1971), **Paris Peasant**, Picador, London, 1980. [Translated by S.W. Taylor] p.1.

2. Western building ceremonies

Introduction

Following a series of lectures by Philip Gibbs on the Malay building process, twenty-nine architecture students from Deakin University were asked to invent a new system of building ceremonies. Here is a compilation of some of their responses:

Before a person buys a block of land he should try to get a feeling for the place by camping there for a while. If he would like to live there permanently he should have the soil tested by an engineer. If the soil proves to be good he should celebrate by having a party with his friends and future neighbours at the block of land. But if the soil proves to be bad he should abandon that block of land and search for another.

* * *

The sale of the block of land should be finalised over a meal paid for by the real estate agent. The buyers should erect a sign on the block of land which states they now own it.

* * *

The owners should roughly plan the house while they are at the block of land. For example, they should decide where the windows should go with respect to views, and locate rooms according to the positions of the sun throughout the day.

* * *

The builder should consult the weather bureau to ensure that work on the house will begin on a fine day. On the morning of the appointed day the owner should provide breakfast for the tradesmen at the block of land. After breakfast he should turn the first sod with a shovel presented to him by the bank that loaned him the money to build the house. Every time a different building trade begins work on the house he should provide food and drink for the tradesmen.

* * *

The owner should prick one of her fingers and let a few drops of blood drip on the foundations. She should bury a personal possession in the foundations before the concrete has set. She should perform numerous firsts, such as hammering the first nail, and laying the first brick. Once the house is finished she should have a party for everyone who helped to build it.

* * *

A priest should bless the house before the owners finally move in. On that night their friends and neighbours should give them a rowdy house-warming party. Everyone who comes to the party should give them a small gift for the new house.

Nearly all of the students recognised that building ceremonies gave people who could not physically build a house for themselves a chance to participate in the building process in a meaningful way. Twenty-seven students invented building ceremonies that involved the owner of the house.

Again, nearly all of the students acknowledged that building ceremonies should be performed throughout the entire building process. Twenty-six students invented building ceremonies that were performed before construction began, twenty-one invented ceremonies that were performed during the course of construction, and twenty invented ceremonies that were performed after construction finished. This in fact reflects what really happens: a ground breaking ceremony is performed before construction begins, a foundation-stone ceremony and a topping ceremony are both performed during the course of constuction, and a completion ceremony is performed after construction finishes.

The students anticipated a surprisingly diverse range of benefits to arise from their building ceremonies. These included comfort, developing a strong bond with a place, friendship, good health, good luck, happiness, knowledge, living in harmony with nature, prosperity, and security. Many Chinese also anticipate similar kinds of things as a result of good feng-shui.

The building ceremonies invented by the students piqued my curiosity. I wondered whether the building ceremonies performed currently in

Australia and other Western countries were as dynamic as the students' imaginary ones. Also I wondered whether any new building ceremonies were evolving in the community.

Ground breaking

The final selection of a site for a building or a town depended once on good omens. The Etruscans, for example, believed the universe lay revealed in the liver, which was divided into sixteen celestial provinces, each ruled by its own god. Priests used the livers of sacrificed animals to divine the planning of cities and other important events. In **The Ten Books on Architecture** Vitruvius advocates the return of hepatoscopy as a method of testing a site for a town:

"Our ancestors, when about to build a town or an army post, sacrificed some of the cattle that were wont to feed on the site proposed and examined their livers. If the livers of the first victims were dark-coloured or abnormal, they sacrificed others, to see whether the fault was due to disease or their food.... If they continued to find it abnormal, they argued from this that the food and water supply found in such a place would be just as unhealthy for man, and so they moved away and changed to another neighbourhood, healthfulness being their chief object."[1]

The siting of Waltham abbey is an interesting example of site selection from the English-speaking world. In the reign of King Canute a man dreamed correctly that a large flint cross was buried on St. Michael's Hill at Montacute in Somerset. The cross, so wondrously revealed, was obviously destined for an important holy centre, but no one knew where. So it was loaded on a wagon pulled by twenty-four oxen, which were allowed to make their own way across country. After many days they stopped at Waltham Cross in Essex, where Waltham Abbey was founded to house the miraculous cross.

In India the site of a house was abandoned if ashes, bones, chaff, hair, red earth, a skull or woodwork from old houses was found while digging the hole for the central post. On the other hand, it was lucky to find brick or stone. I suspect the ground breaking ceremony currently practised widely in the West was once something like this. Significantly, I think, a religious official in ancient Rome who foretold the future by interpreting omens is called an 'a-u-g-u-r', while a large tool for boring holes deep in the ground is called an 'a-u-g-e-r'.

No more is a ground breaking ceremony performed to discover whether a site is lucky. Instead it merely signifies the start of the building process, which, of course, is still an important function. In **House** Tracy Kidder describes a modern ground breaking 'ceremony':

"The first pass the machine makes over the ground, ripping the hair off the earth, looks like an act of great violence. The bulldozer does resemble a beast, but the creature is both unruly and extremely methodical. Gradually, the sense of disruption goes out of the scene. The machine makes its first cuts. It goes back over the same suddenly dark ground. Piles of earth mount up. The hole deepens and, as sand appears, turns orange. Watching the bulldozer work is restful and mesmerizing. Its noise discourages speech, leaving each of the party alone and thoughtful for moments."[2]

Ground breaking ceremonies are usually informal occasions. Although it was probably more informal than most, take for example the ground breaking ceremony for Australia's old Parliament House, which was held on August 28, 1923. "The space which had been set apart for the function became so crowded that it became a problem of keeping the ground clear for the chief actors in the piece," reported the *Sydney Morning Herald*. "Finally a Press photographer took charge of the situation, although no one knew him as such. In commanding tones he told the crowd, conspicuous among whom were an army of children, that the proceedings could not commence until they moved back. This had the desired effect."[3] *Figure 49*, which is based on a newspaper photograph of the ceremony, shows a large, disorderly crowd milling around a flagpole and the steam shovel used to turn the first sod by Mr Stewart, the Federal Minister for Works and Railways at that time.

In 1986 I designed a ground breaking ceremony for the Belconnen Community Centre in Canberra, which was never performed, unfortunately. It was loosely based on the two ground breaking ceremonies for Australia's new Parliament House. In keeping with tradition, it was informal and involved augury. But most importantly, it was meant to

Figure 49

echo throughout the entire building process and beyond. Following is an annotated brief outline of the programme:

A string quartet plays music as people arrive at the site.

Music is often part of a ground breaking ceremony. At the first ground breaking ceremony for new Parliament House a military band played "Hey Big Spender," which turned out to be prophetic because the building finally cost over one billion dollars.

The guest of honour is introduced, then he makes a short speech.

Usually an important person performs a ground breaking ceremony, which certainly adds to the auspiciousness of the event, and also helps to reinforce the event's importance. Both ground breaking ceremonies for new Parliament House were performed by the Prime Minister at that time, Mr. Fraser.

The guest of honour is made an honorary member of a building trade union.

This reinforces the fact that a ground breaking ceremony is a builder's ceremony. Indeed, it is required sometimes by a trade union. At the second ground breaking ceremony for new Parliament House Mr. Fraser was awarded temporary membership in the Federated Engine Drivers and Firemen's Association, which also represents bulldozer drivers. He then cleared a forty metre strip of land with a bulldozer, which got work started officially.

The guest of honour turns the first sod using a special spade, fills a small plastic bag and a flower pot with soil from the first sod, and then plants a seed in the flower pot.

At the first ground breaking ceremony for new Parliament House Mr. Fraser turned the first sod with a silver spade. At the Belconnen ceremony I wanted the guest of honour to use an ordinary spade with "Turning the First Sod, Belconnen Community Centre" and the date painted on the blade. This could have been mounted and given to the guest of honour as a souvenir after the ceremony.

The bag of soil could have been placed in the Centre's foundation-stone when it was laid. If the seed had grown in the soil from the first sod, which would have been a good omen, it could have been planted in the ground at the Centre's opening ceremony.

In 1984 I designed a ceremony to celebrate moves to establish a Sherlock Holmes Centre at the University of Minnesota. Although it was not a ground breaking ceremony - no site existed - it was another type of pre-construction ceremony. Three distinguished Sherlock Holmes scholars had great fun making impressions of their hands and feet in wet cement. *Figure 50.* "You are invited to witness Michael Harrison, E.W. McDiarmid and John Bennett Shaw take the first 'concrete steps' toward a Sherlock Holmes Centre at the University of Minnesota," read the invitation card. The slabs of concrete will be laid in the lobby during the Centre's opening ceremony.

Figure 50

Foundation-stones

A foundation-stone is an inscribed block of stone laid in a wall of a public building near ground level, which marks the centre of the world (I explain what I mean by this later on). It is sometimes laid on another block of stone called a 'foot-stone', which is usually hollow and contains historical documents and symbolical objects called 'foundation deposits'. Nowadays, however, it is more common for the foundation-stone to be hollow and to contain the foundation deposits. A foundation-stone is often laid at the northeast corner of a building (hence sometimes it is called a cornerstone), because in the northern hemisphere the sun rises in the northeast on June 24 - the day dedicated to Saint John, the patron saint of stone masons. A foundation-stone was once truly part of a building's foundations, but nowadays it is usually a symbol only, since most modern buildings have foundations of concrete and not stone.

At a typical foundation-stone ceremony, the owner of the building under constuction welcomes the official party, and introduces the architect to the person invited to lay the stone. Usually an important person lays the foundation-stone at an auspicious time, which helps to reinforce the event's importance. For example, the foundation-stone of City Hall in Philadelphia was laid by the leader of the Freemasons in Pennsylvania on American Independence Day, July 4, 1874; and the foundation-stone of the Shrine of Rememberance in Melbourne was laid by the Governor of Victoria on Armistice Day, November 11, 1927.

The architect hands the person invited to lay the foundation-stone a trowel and a mallet, which often are highly symbolical objects. For example, 'Allgood' - a hardware manufacturer - produces a trowel that is symbolical of building masonry, the pointed arch, and the secrets of column entasis. Alan Tye, who designed the trowel, said even some of the shadows it casts are also symbolic.[4] *Figure 51.* Another example is the mallet the Prince of Wales used at the foundation-stone ceremony of the Capitol building in Canberra. It was made of fifty different varieties of Australian timbers, each State of Australia having supplied its quota. *Figure 52.* At the end of a typical foundation-stone ceremony, the trowel or the mallet is given to the person who laid the stone as a souvenir.

Figures 51–52

The person laying the foundation-stone spreads some mortar with the trowel, then places a new coin in the bed of mortar. The foundation-stone is lowered into position, and the architect and the builder make certain it is level. The person laying the foundation-stone strikes each corner of the stone three times with the mallet, starting at the top, right-hand corner, and moving in an anticlockwise direction. At the same time he says: "In equity, justice, temperance and fortitude, I declare this stone well and truly laid." The owner of the building places the foundation deposits in a cavity in the foundation-stone, which is then sealed with a metal plate. The foundation-stone ceremony concludes with a prayer of dedication or the National Anthem or both.

Over the years the Church has helped to perpetuate foundation-stone lore in particular, because the foundation-stone is a symbol of Christ. For example, one popular Christian hymn begins: "Christ is made the sure foundation, Christ the head and cornerstone." A foundation-stone is also symbolically significant for Freemasons, because it is the one remaining link between themselves and the craftsmen or 'operative' masons. It was once quite common for Freemasons to perform the foundation-stone ceremonies of public buildings, such as town halls, because they were considered the guardians of esoteric building knowledge. *Figure 53.*

Figure 53

Inscriptions

While most inscriptions on foundation-stones give the name of the person who laid the foundation-stone and the date, some give much more information. For example, the inscription on the foundation-stone of City Hall in Philadelphia also lists the organisations represented at the foundation-stone ceremony, and the names of the guest speaker, the architect, the builder, the members of the building committee, and several important government officials. Not only is the length of this inscription unusual, but also the way it is rendered: "The letters are about an inch in size, deeply cut, and the initial letter of each name is coloured red, while the remainder of the text is in blue. This with the white of the marble, gives the national colours."[5]

When this particular foundation-stone was laid, Benjamin Harris Brewster addressed the crowd, declaring: "This work which we now do...will...in some far off future day be all that remains to tell the story of our civilization, and to testify to the dignity and public spirit of our people."[6] This is a common sentiment at a foundation-stone ceremony. It suggests, in other words, that a foundation-stone should survive the ravages of time and leave for posterity a record of a building and the era when it was built. Edgar Allan Poe certainly had some fun with this idea in his short-story *Mellonta Tauta*. In the year 2848 some archaeologists discover a foundation-stone which bears the following inscription:

"This Corner Stone of a Monument to the
Memory of
GEORGE WASHINGTON
was laid with appropriate ceremonies on the
19TH DAY OF OCTOBER, 1847,
the anniversary of the surrender of
Lord Cornwallis
to General Washington at Yorktown,
A.D. 1781,
under the auspices of the
Washington Monument Association of the
city of New York"[7]

The archaeologists make several erroneous deductions from this inscription: "From the few words thus preserved, we glean several important items of knowledge, not the least interesting of which is the fact that a thousand years ago *actual* monuments had fallen into disuse - as was all very proper - the people contenting themselves, as we do now, with a mere indication of the design to erect a monument at some future time; a corner-stone being cautiously laid by itself...as a guarantee of the magnanimous *intention.** We ascertain, too, very distinctly, from this admirable inscription, the how as well as the where and the what, of the great surrender in question. As to the *where,* it was Yorktown (wherever that was), and as to the *what,* it was General Cornwallis (no doubt some wealthy dealer in corn). *He* was surrendered. The inscription commemorates the surrender of - what? - why, 'of Lord Cornwallis'. The only question is what could the savages wish him surrendered for. But when we remember that these savages were undoubtedly cannibals, we are led to the conclusion that they intended him for sausage. As to the *how* of the surrender, no language can be more explicit. Lord Cornwallis was surrendered (for sausage) 'under the auspices of the Washington Monument Association' - no doubt a charitable institution for the depositing of corner-stones."[8]

The Pioneer 10 spacecraft was fitted with an inscribed metal plaque, designed to show scientifically educated inhabitants of some other star system when the spacecraft was launched, from where, and by what kind of beings. *Figure 54.* The aliens who eventually intercept the spacecraft will probably have as much, if not more, trouble interpreting this inscription as the archaeologists had in Edgar Allan Poe's story.

The centre of the world

Many cultures believed the forces of nature took the form of a serpent, and the place where it was fixed to the earth was the centre of the world. Such an important place was usually marked by a stone, a shrine, or some other structure. For example, the place where Python was buried

---

* Life does imitate art. In 1920 the Prince of Wales made a similar comment about Canberra. He said: "I think that at the present moment Canberra consists chiefly of foundation-stones." *The Sydney Morning Herald,* June 22, 1920.

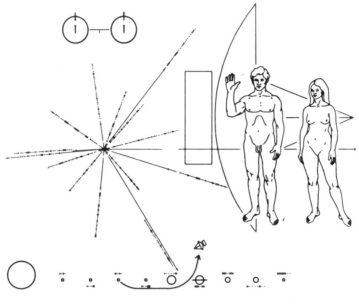

Figure 54

in Delphi was the centre of the ancient Greek world, which was marked by a conically shaped stone, called an omphalos. The word 'omphalos' is now used generally to describe any divined, geomantic centre.

It may be that a foundation-stone is a symbol of a sacred stone, such as the Omphalos of Delphi. In England, for example, sacred stones were built into the foundations of several old churches. Whatever its origins, a foundation-stone is laid at the centre of the world. In India a mason drives a stake through the head of the serpent that supports the world, fixing it securely to the earth. He then lays a foundation-stone over the stake, which is at the centre of the world. Philip Thompson, an architecture student at RMIT, describes in more detail the climax of a traditional Vedic, foundation-stone ceremony that was performed at the site of the Hare Krishna temple at Bambra on December 31, 1988:

"A tiny golden statue of Ananta Sesha - the snake that supports the world - was put inside a glass cube. This was placed on a specially purified brick at the botom of a pit two metres deep, with Ananta Sesha facing east. This was what everyone had come to see: Ananta Sesha

Figure 55

installed to support the foundation of the temple. *Figure 55*. Ananta Sesha was worshipped with incense and flowers, then the president of the temple half-filled the pit with concrete."

However, laying a foundation-stone at the centre of the world is not an ancient or a non-Western practice only. For example, the foundation-stone of the Capitol building was laid at the centre of the world in Australia. The inscription on top of the foundation-stone reads:

> "His Royal Highness,
> Edward, Prince of Wales,
> Laid this stone 21 June,
> 1920."

A dot placed in the middle of the letter 'o' in the word 'of' indicated the exact centre of Canberra - Australia's capital city and, symbolically, the centre of the world in Australia. The foundation-stone was moved because the Capitol building was never completed. Instead, Australia's new Parliament House was eventually built on the site. Thus the huge flagpole on top of Parliament House now marks the centre of the world in Australia. *Figure 56.* It is certainly appropriate for a flagpole - a symbol of the axis mundi - to mark the centre of the world. A replica of the flagpole on top of Parliament House also marks the geographical centre of Australia (latitude: 25°36' 36·4" south; longitude 134°21' 17·3" east), which is an unremarkable patch of scrub in the Northern Territory.

Once people walked in procession to a foundation-stone ceremony, which helped to reinforce the idea that a foundation-stone was

Figure 56

laid at the centre of the world: "Every road can symbolise the 'road of life,' and any walk a 'pilgrimage,' a peregrination to the centre of the world."[9] In the foundation-stone ceremony of the Town Hall in Leeds in 1853, the procession included a number of brass bands, the vicar, the architect, the soldiers stationed in Leeds, the committees of the Philosophical and Literary Society and the Mechanics' Institutes, the Friendly Societies, the Guardians of the Poor, representatives of business and the professions, members of the Town Council, and visitors from other West Riding boroughs. A procession like this one is very rare nowadays.

Speeches also help to reinforce the idea that a foundation-stone is laid at the centre of the world. For example, Benjamin Harris Brewster, speaking at the foundation-stone ceremony of City Hall in Philadelphia, declared: "[City Hall] is placed ...at the centre of human concourse from which all things radiate and to which all things converge."[10] He also suggested that the city of Philadelphia was the centre of America:

"In those sad days [during the American revolution] here came, as to a common centre, all of the wise and brave who guided and led in that contest."[11] The centre of the world was often the place of an oracle, and speeches like Brewster's maintain this oracular tradition still.

Such an important place as the centre of the world must have an impressive and, most importantly, a permanent marker. City Hall in Philadelphia, for example, Brewster described as: "...one of the most majestic and useful structures that adorn... any city of the world. MAY IT LAST FOR EVER!"[12] On the other hand, Australia's old Parliament House in Canberra, which is a modest building, designed to last only fifty or sixty years, has no foundation-stone. Perhaps it was thought that such a temporary building was not worthy of marking the centre of the world? In many American towns the first courthouse was constructed on a corner of the central town square, or on land across the street, so that the central place was saved for the permanent building that was to follow.

Foundation deposits

Once people buried a human sacrifice under the foundations of a building because they believed the building would collapse if the forces of nature were not sufficiently placated. For example, the Dyaks of Borneo used to suspend the main post of a house over a deep hole, throw a young girl into the hole, and cut the rope holding the post, crushing the girl to death. Similar beliefs and customs also existed in Western cultures, and people were buried alive in the foundations of bridges, castles, churches, houses and town walls well into the second millennium. For example, Saint Columba had a monk named Oran buried alive under the foundations of his abbey on the island of Iona, because the spirits of the soil demolished by night what he had built by day.

According to folklore, twelve stone masons walled up a little girl in the ramparts of Copenhagen, while her cries of alarm were drowned by loud music. Music, by the way, is still played at a typical foundation-stone ceremony. For example, "Christ is made the sure foundation,

Christ the head and corner stone" is sung at a typical Anglican foundation-stone ceremony; "Advance Australia Fair" and "Waltzing Matilda" were played at the foundation-stone ceremony of Parliament House in Canberra; and "Corner Stone March" was played at the foundation-stone ceremony of City Hall in Philadelphia, having been composed specially for the occasion.

When the old church at Holsworth in Devon was restored in 1885, a skeleton was found embedded in the south-west angle of the wall. The victim appeared to have been buried alive, because his mouth had been gagged with a handful of mortar, and stones had been hastily piled about his corpse.

Even though people are no longer buried alive under the foundations of buildings, this gruesome practice still remains in our consciousness. In 1989 Mark Lynch, a political cartoonist for *The Australian*, compared the political 'sacrifice' of the then Minister for Aviation Support, Gary Punch, with a foundation-stone sacrifice. The Australian Government had decided to build an extra runway at Sydney airport, despite strong

Figure 57

opposition from Mr. Punch, who represented people living in the airport's flight path. Lynch's cartoon showed Prime Minister Bob Hawke pouring a truck load of concrete over Mr. Punch, while saying: "It's only appropriate that I lay the foundation block!"[13] *Figure 57.*

A foundation sacrifice not only placated the forces of nature, but also provided a building with a spirit. Thus the white ladies and luminous children rumoured to appear in certain old houses may be, in fact, the ghosts of the victims buried under the foundations of those houses. This association was exploited in a newspaper advertisement for reinforced concrete slab foundations, which featured a photograph of a haunted house and the caption: "Things that go bump in the night." The point of the advertisement was that a house on reinforced concrete slab foundations does not creak like a house on stumps.[14] *Figure 58.*

Figure 58

Animal sacrifices eventually replaced human ones. Of the many kinds of animals sacrificed, the most common were cats, dogs, fowl (including eggs), horses, oxen and sheep. For example, in Denmark a lamb - no doubt chosen for its Christian symbolism - was buried under the altar of a church to ensure the building would not collapse; and in modern Greece the blood of a cock or a ram or a lamb was poured over a foundation-stone, then the animal was buried underneath the stone.

The ornamentation on ancient Greek temples was meant to recall foundation sacrifices and the implements of sacrifice, says George Hersey in **The Lost Meaning of Classical Architecture**.[15] For example, he suggests that a triglyph represented three upright bones wrapped top and bottom with strands of dripping fat; and a tympanum was named after a drum made from bones and animal skins, which also doubled sometimes as a sacrificial table.

Foundation deposits eventually replaced animal sacrifices, at least in most Western countries. For example, old and worn out shoes have been found walled up in many old houses in southern England and Wales. Old and worn out shoes were regarded once as powerful lucky charms. The tradition of tying old shoes to the back of a motor car at a wedding for good luck sometimes still occurs.

Figure 59

Squat, round-bellied, stoneware bottles bearing the face of a bearded man and a crest or a cipher have also been found walled up in many old English houses. *Figure 59.* They were commonly known as witch bottles because they contained powerful charms to combat witchcraft, such as iron nails, twisted wire, human hair, nail parings, pieces of cloth or felt studded with pins, and urine.

Some builders still conceal objects and messages in the houses they build. Jim Locke, one of the builders Tracy Kidder writes about in **House**, wrote in lumber crayon, on a scrap of crown molding:

"This House Built
for Jonathan and Judith
Souweine
May - Sept. 1983
By:
Apple Corps Builders
Apple Valley
Ashfield, Mass.
For $146,000
By:
Alex Ghiselin
Richard Gougeon

Edward Krutsky
Jim Locke
June 18, 1983"

Tracy Kidder says:

"Jim nails the piece of molding in a corner where, once the house is done, no one but another builder doing repair work is likely to find it. It's a note adrift in a bottle, a message sent across time to another carpenter who does not yet exist but who will perhaps understand the gesture and appreciate the work."[16]

Coins, documents, newspapers and photographs are commonly buried under a foundation-stone nowadays. Besides serving as the spirit of a building, these articles are also intended for a future witness and reference, which is rather bizarre, for surely the hope of everyone at a foundation-stone ceremony is that the stone will never be removed.

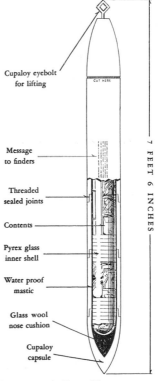

The burial of foundation deposits sometimes occurs outside of a foundation-stone ceremony. For example, the Time Capsule buried on the site of the New York World's Fair is meant to show people in the year 6939 how people in the year 1938 lived. Stored inside a torpedo-shaped container $7\frac{1}{2}$ feet long and $8\frac{3}{8}$ inches in diameter are thirty-five everyday objects, seventy-five samples of common materials, three and a half small reels of microfilm, and three newsreels. *Figure 60*. In **World's Fair** E.L. Doctorow describes some of these articles:

"...a windup alarm clock, a can opener, and a toothbrush and a can of tooth

Figure 60

powder and a Mickey Mouse plastic cup, and a hat by Lilly Daché; and they had put in material like asbestos and coal, and messages from scientists, and a U.S. silver dollar and the alphabet in hand-set type, and an electric wall switch; and they had put in the Lord's Prayer in three hundred languages, and a dictionary and photographs of factories and assembly lines, and assorted comic strips and **Gone with the Wind**, by Margaret Mitchell...and finally newsreels of President Roosevelt giving a speech, and scenes of the United States Navy on maneuvers and the Japanese bombing of Canton in the war with China, and a fashion show in Miami, Florida."[17]

The meaning of foundation deposits may be misinterpreted by people in the future, just as the inscription was on the foundation-stone in *Mellonta Tauta*. Doctorow writes:

"My father wondered aloud what the people five thousand years from now would derive from these things collected in the Time Capsule. 'They will think we were good engineers for a primitive people,' he said, 'and had in our religion only one prayer, which we spoke in a babble of tongues, and that we wore odd hats and murdered each other and read abominable books.'"[18]

The burial of the Time Capsule resembled a foundation-stone ceremony in several respects. For example, an important person buried the Time Capsule at an auspicious time, and music played as it was lowered into the ground. In *The story of the Time Capsule* G. Edward Pendray writes:

"It was lowered 50 feet into the earth on the site of the Westinghouse Building at the grounds of the World's Fair at high noon on September 23, 1938, the precise moment of the autumal equinox. While a Chinese gong tolled solemnly, A.W. Robertson, chairman of the board of the Westinghouse Electric & Manufacturing Co., committed the Time Capsule to posterity with these words: 'May the Time Capsule sleep well. When it is awakened 5,000 years from now, may its contents be found a suitable gift to our far-off descendants.'"[19]

A Chinese gong seems a strange choice of musical instrument under the circumstances, but perhaps one of the organisers had read **The Flying Chinaman** by Harry H. Fein. In this book Nu Chi beats a copper pan to scare away the unfriendly demons who gather around when her husband, Sing High, brags to Sun Sink Soon.[20] People often talk big at an important occasion like the burial of the Time Capsule.

I was very disappointed that no foundation deposits were buried under the foundation-stone of Australia's new Parliament House, which was laid on October 4, 1983. Lost was the opportunity to endow Australia's premier building with a special spirit. I wanted to ask several celebrated Australians to contribute a small object each, such as Patrick White's pen, Sir Donald Bradman's cricket cap, Sir Russell Drysdale's paint-brush, Dawn Fraser's swimsuit, and a pair of Dame Edna Everage's spectacles. Foundation deposits like these would have also reflected the original plans for the site. Walter Burley Griffin, the architect who designed the city of Canberra, earmarked the site for the Capitol build-ing, which would have housed the records of Australian achievement and the archives of the nation, had it been built.

In **Builders' Rites and Ceremonies** G.W. Speth neatly summarises the meaning and the evolution of foundation sacrifices:

"Our forefathers...buried a living human sacrifice in the [foundations] to ensure the stability of the structure; their sons substituted an animal; their sons again a mere effigy or other symbol; and we, their children, still immure a substitute, coins bearing the effigy...of the one person to whom we all are most loyal, and whom we all most love, our Gracious Queen [i.e. Queen Victoria]. I do not assert that one in a hundred is conscious of what he is doing...but the fact remains that unconsciously we are following the customs of our fathers, and symbolically providing a soul for the stucture."[21]

Detective stories

The coincidence between burying a human sacrifice under the founda-tions of a building to placate the forces of nature on the one hand, and burying someone under the foundations of a building to hide a murder on the other, has inspired many detective stories or incidents in them. For example, I believe it inspired *The Musgrave Ritual* -a Sherlock Holmes story - written by Sir Arthur Conan Doyle.[22]

Richard Brunton-the butler at Hurlstone Manor - found the ancient crown of the Kings of England and several old coins in a squat wooden box, hidden in a hole seven feet deep and four feet square, under the cellar floor.[23] It was probably Sir Ralph Musgrave - a prominent Cavalier, and the right-hand man of Charles the Second in his wanderings - who hid them there for safekeeping. But why was the hole so deep if just for a squat wooden box? That it was originally dug to bury alive a human sacrifice in the foundations of Hurlstone is the most likely explanation.

Figure 61

I believe Sir Ralph Musgrave discovered the hole and its ghastly contents while Hurlstone was being renovated, and nobly removed the body to a cemetery. Later he put the squat wooden box containing the crown and the coins in the hole. As symbolical objects, the crown and the coins were certainly appropriate substitutes for a human sacrifice. Perhaps this coincidence caused Sir Ralph to remember the hole when he was searching for a hiding place. The hole's gruesome, original purpose was eventually reinstated when Brunton was buried alive in the hole by his ex-lover, Rachel Howells. Brunton's death was somewhat ironic, for no sooner had he removed the crown than he was buried alive like the human sacrifice the crown had replaced. *Figure 61*.

It is rather surprising that no one saw a ghost in *The Musgrave Ritual* because a foundation sacrifice also provided a building with a spirit. However, in **Sherlock Holmes Faces Death** - the Basil Rathbone and Nigel Bruce film based on *The Musgrave Ritual* - Hurlstone is depicted as being haunted. The local innkeeper grimly warns:

"If those old walls could speak, they'd tell you things that would raise the hair on your head. There are folks hereabouts swear they've seen corpse-lights round the greenhouse, and heard a wailing like lost souls in the limewalk."[24]

Sherlock Holmes Faces Death is one of the best of the Rathbone-Bruce films, partly because of the wonderful sense of mystery and gloom that shrouds Hurlstone. No wonder Dr. Watson describes Hurlstone as "very spooky," and Sherlock Holmes observes: "Houses, like people, have definite personalities and this place is positively ghoulish."[25]

Several incidents in **Hawksmoor** by Peter Ackroyd were also inspired by the darker side of foundation-stone lore.[26] For example, architect Nicholas Dyer murders a beggar and a quantity-surveyor, then hides their bodies in the foundations of two churches he has designed. On the one hand Dyer's churches need a foundation sacrifice, and on the other he is a psychopathic killer. Several incidents in **The Mystery of Edwin Drood** by Charles Dickens were similarly inspired. For example, the narrator wonders: "...whether [any nuns] were ever walled up alive in odd angles and jutting gables of the [Nuns' House] for having some ineradicable leaven of busy mother Nature in them...."[27] Finally, it appears that **The Mysteries of the Court of London** by G.W.M. Reynolds, and **The Bradys' Strangest Case** by Francis Doughty are two more examples, judging by one illustration from each story reproduced in **The Art of Mystery & Detective Stories** by Peter Haining.[28] *Figure 62.*

Topping ceremonies

Many people once believed that unless the tree spirits which lived in the timber frame of a house were propitiated with some kind of sacrifice when the roof was completed, they would eventually make trouble for the owner of the house. For example, the Toradjas and the Tonapoo - two tribes from Central Celebes - both believed this. In **The Golden Bough** Sir James Frazer writes:

"...when a new dwelling is ready the Toradjas...kill a goat, a pig, or a buffalo, and smear all the woodwork with its blood. If the building is a *lobo* or spirit-house a fowl or a dog is killed on the ridge of the roof, and its blood allowed to flow down on both sides. The ruder Tonapoo in such cases sacrifice a human being on the roof."[29]

Fig. 62

Many people in the West also believed that the roof of a building would eventually be damaged by wind and lightning if Wodin and Thor were not appeased with a sacrifice of some kind when either the frame of the roof or the roof itself was completed. For example, in **Hawksmoor** architect Nicholas Dyer describes the topping of the tower of his church at Spittle-Fields:

"...it is the Custom in our Nation to have the Mason's son lay the highest and last stone on the top of the Tower its Lanthorn.... He was in great good Humour on the Morning of his Ascent and saw it as a merry Enterprize, climbing out upon the wooden Scaffold and nimbly advancing his Steps to the Tower. The Labourers and the Mason, his Father, look'd up at him and call'd out *How do you Tom?* and *One step further!* and such like Observations, while I stood silent.... But there was a sudden Gust of Wind and the Boy, now close to the Lanthorn, seemed to lose Heart as the Clowds scudded above his Head. He gazed steadily at me for an Instant and I cryed, *Go on! Go on!;* and at this Moment, just as he was coming up to the spiry Turret, the timbers of the Scaffold, being insecurely plac'd or rotten, cracked asunder and the Boy missed his Footing and fell from the Tower....

"The Mason his Father calling for Help rushed in the direction of...where now Thomas lay, and the Work men followed amaz'd. But he had expir'd at once.... Then the Father made to unbuckle his son's shoes...but I led him away and spoke to him gently. At any rate, *I said,* give him leave to be buried where he fell and according to Custom: to which in his Agony he assented....

"And so all this was given to my Purpose: there is a certain ridiculous Maxim that The Church loves not Blood but this is nothing to the Case for the Eucharist must be mingled with Blood. Thus had I found the Sacrifice desir'd in the Spittle-Fields, and not at my own Hands...."[30]

Here a human sacrifice was buried where he fell. But sometimes the victim's body was immurred directly under the roof of a building. For example, according to the Olympic historian Aristarchus, the body of a dead man dressed in armour was found in the roof of the Temple of Juno.

Similarly, mummified cats have been found in the roofs of many old buildings in England. Perhaps the best known example is the so-called "Sudbury cat" which was discovered in the roof of an old watermill at Sudbury in 1971. Several distasters occurred at the mill after the cat had been removed, including the collapse of the roof. There was no more trouble after the cat was replaced where it was found, along with a letter of apology for having disturbed its rest. This curious string of events convinced some people that the cat was the mill's guardian spirit.

A mummified cat holding a mummified rat in its jaws was found in the roof of an old shop in the West-end of London. The animals were subsequently fixed to a card and displayed in the window of the shop. *Figure 63.* In *Shopkeepers' Advertising Novelties,* James Scott suggests this particular pair of animals was hardly unique.[31]

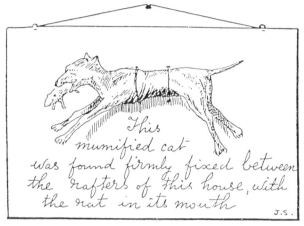

Figure 63

Sometimes the victim's head was cut off and fixed to the roof of a building. In Germany the skulls of horses were often placed over the ends of bargeboards - where they crossed at the ridge. (The horse is particularly sacred to Wodin, as the goat is to Thor.) Heads fixed to the roofs of buildings served other functions besides placating Wodin and Thor: they were consulted as oracles (the expressions "look a gift-horse in the mouth" and "straight from the horse's mouth" come from consulting a horse's head); they protected houses from evil spirits and pestilence; and they protected the ends of some of the roof timbers from the weather.

Symbols eventually replaced humans and animals as sacrifices. For example, gargoyles are stone effigies of human and animal sacrifices once offered to Wodin and Thor. *Figure 64.* Likewise are many corbels, festoons, finials, ridge tiles, urns and weathervanes.

In Norway evergreen wreaths decorated with flowers and silk ribbons replaced humans and animals as sacrifices. In **The Master Builder** by

Henrik Ibsen, Hilde Wangel remembers the topping ceremony for a church which Halvard Solness, the master builder, once performed:

Figure 64

"There was a band in the churchyard. And hundreds and hundreds of people. We schoolgirls were dressed in white. And all of us had flags.... Then you climbed straight up the scaffolding. Right to the very top. And you had a big wreath with you. And you hung that wreath right on the top of the weathercock.... It was wonderfully exciting, standing down there and looking up at you. Imagine now - if he were to fall! The master builder himself!"[32]

Elsewhere, baskets of fruit, bunches of flowers, and trees also replaced humans and animals as sacrifices. For example, at a traditional German house or barn raising, a freshly cut evergreen tree decorated with gilded paper, ornaments and ribbons was attached to the gable of the building under construction for Wodin's horse to eat. *Figure 65*. In the light of this custom, which has spread to many other countries, it is interesting that both the ridge pole and the roof itself are sometimes referred to as the 'rooftree'.

The similarity between "a freshly cut evergreen tree decorated with gilded paper, ornaments and ribbons" and a Christmas tree is certainly not a coincidence: with the advent of Christianity, Wodin was displaced by Saint Nicholas or Father Christmas, who also inherited some of Wodin's symbols. The fact that roofs are part of Wodin's domain may also explain why Father Christmas climbs down chimneys.

German-style topping ceremonies are still performed in many Western countries, although nowadays it appears they are more common for skyscrapers than for houses, at least in Australia and the United States. *Figures 66 & 67*. This is to be expected, however, since skyscrapers are much taller than houses, and therefore are more likely to offend Wodin and Thor. The following topping ceremony for a house was performed by the builders Tracy Kidder writes about in **House:**

Fig. 65

"Ned takes a white pine bough from the woods beside the brook, and he carries it up the ladder.... He stands on tiptoes on the scaffold under the ridge and reaches up towards the top of the house, the greenery in one hand.... Alex and Richard have their backs turned at this moment. When they look at the house again, Ned has come back to the ground and the tree is up."[33]

In **An Early American Home and the Fun We Had Building It,** Claude H. Miller explains the utilitarian purpose of this custom from the point of view of the owner of a new house:

"...the green tree means that the future owner is expected to appear the next Saturday at the time when the men quit work and pass around the [cigars]. It is good business to do this. In the final analysis your house is at the mercy of your workmen. If a cigar or two will make them think the owner is a good guy they may make their mitres a little more carefully or drive screws with a screw driver instead of a hammer."[34]

Figure 66   *Figure 67*

A topping ceremony for a skyscraper is often much more elaborate than one for a house. Take for example the topping ceremony for Momentum Place - one of the tallest buildings in Dallas, Texas - performed on October 7, 1986. Employees and executives of the three companies involved in the project signed the last steel beam to complete the building's skeletal frame. A pine tree and the flags of the United States and Texas were attached to the beam. As it was hoisted to the top of the building to be set in place, four thousand helium-filled balloons were released into the air. "[The ceremony] was to appease the gods, to indicate the builder would go no further into the heavens," one of the developers of the building explained.[35] After the ceremony, the construction workers had a party in a nearby parking lot.

Raisings

House and barn raisings were not merely working bees, but also important social events. Indeed, the freshly cut evergreen tree for

Wodin's horse to eat also indicated that a party would conclude the day's work, which is where a barn dance and the expression "raising the roof" both come from. In **Letters from an American Farmer**, J. Hector St. John de Crevecour describes the house-raising for "Andrew the Hebridean":

"As [Andrew] had neither mowing nor reaping to do that year, I told him that the time was come to build his house; and that for the purpose I would myself invite the neighbourhood to a frolic; that thus he would have a large dwelling erected and some upland cleared in one day. Mr. P.R., his old friend, came at the time appointed, with all his hands, and brought victuals in plenty; I did the same. About forty people repaired to the spot; the songs and merry stories went round the woods from cluster to cluster, as the people had gathered to their different works; trees fell on all sides, bushes were cut up and heaped; and while many were thus employed, others with their teams hauled the big logs to the spot which Andrew had pitched upon for the erection of his new dwelling. We all dined in the woods; in the afternoon, the logs were placed with skids and the usual contrivances; thus the rude house was raised and above two acres of land cut up, cleared, and heaped.

"Whilst all these different operations were performing, Andrew was absolutely incapable of working; it was to him the most solemn holiday he had ever seen; it would have been sacrilegious of him to have defiled it with menial labour. Poor man, he sanctified it with joy and thanksgiving and honest libations: he went from one to the other with the bottle in his hand, pressing everybody to drink, and drinking himself to show the example. He spent the whole day in smiling, laughing, and

Figure 68

uttering monosyllables.... The powerful lord, the wealthy merchant, on seeing the superb mansion finished, never can feel half the joy and real happiness which was felt and enjoyed on that day by this honest Hebridean, though this new dwelling, erected in the midst of the woods, was nothing more than a square inclosure, composed of twenty-four large, clumsy logs, let in at the ends. When the work was finished, the company made the woods resound with the noise of their three cheers and the honest wishes they formed for Andrew's prosperity. He could say nothing, but with thankful tears he shook hands with them all. Thus, from the first day he had landed [in America], Andrew marched towards this important event...."[36] *Figure 68.*

Figures 69–72

Most people do not actively participate in the building process like this any more, because they have neither the skill nor the time to build their own house. But in Australia many people do make their own letterbox, which often is their house in miniature. *Figures 69-72.* This is a very important task, I believe, because it gives people a second chance to actively participate in the building process. Witold Rybczynski is right

- the most beautiful house in the world is the one that you build for yourself.[37]

Opening ceremonies

A new public building is opened usually by an important person, often at an auspicious time. The important person customarily cuts a ribbon strung across the main entrance, or opens the front door with a ceremonial key. At the opening ceremony of Australia's old Parliament House, Prime Minister Bruce handed the front door key of Parliament House to the Duke of York, who opened the building on the stroke of 11 o'clock on May 9, 1927 - the twenty-sixth anniversary of the opening of Australia's first Parliament. The Prime Minister presented the Duke with a souvenir golden key and casket, and handed the President of the Senate and the Speaker of the House of Representatives the keys of Parliament House. The actual key used by the Duke was placed in the archives of Parliament House as a memento of the occasion.

Many people have a 'house-warming' party when they move into a house. I clearly remember the one for my parents' house, about twenty-five years ago. A group of my parents' friends arrived banging saucepans with wooden spoons and throwing stones on the roof, which now I realize was to scare away any evil spirits. In **An Early American Home and the Fun We Had Building It**, Claude H. Miller explains why a house-warming is a good idea:

"On such an occasion, you will receive such an earful of praise and congratulation that it will make you like your home better every day you live in it. A house-warming in a chicken coop would be a success. There is something about new wood and the smell of fresh paint with everything spic and span that makes even the most conservative guest grunt: 'Pretty nice ranch, Bill.' If you are really proud of your home you get the thrill that comes once in a lifetime when you show it to your friends."[38]

An opening ceremony may be designed to suit the character of a particular building. For example, between May 29 and June 6, 1899, three separate events were staged to celebrate the opening of a new warehouse in Melbourne which was owned by Frederick Thomas Sargood, a softgoods merchant. Firstly, the building's innovative fire services were demonstrated publicly:

"...when the water was turned on the miniature cataracts spouted from all the pipes and the water poured down the external face of the building in copious volume. The sprinklers inside the building were also brought into use, and poured quantities of water from the jets, while the automatic fire alarm continued to ring loudly."[39]

Secondly, a "smoke concert" was held in the Melbourne Town Hall for the 900 workmen and artisans who constructed the warehouse, which involved musical entertainment and a free supply of refreshments, cigars and tobacco. Finally, 2500 customers and commercial travellers attended a preview of the firm's softgoods at the new warehouse.

Figure 73

Before my friend Sherry Rose-Bond moved into an old house she bought in Philadelphia, she organized a working bee of her friends to paint the inside of the house. After they had finished painting they had a party and everyone signed the inside of the coat-cupboard door for posterity. (This ceremony also has some points in common with both a topping ceremony - especially the one for Momentum Place in Dallas, Texas - and a house-raising.)

If ever I design a brick house with patterned walls, I hope that while it is being built a member of the family will knit similarly patterned pullovers for everyone in the household. (It is possible to produce the same pattern in both brick work and knitting because laying brick after brick, row upon row, is a similar process to knitting stitch after stitch, row upon row. *Figure 73.*) Then just before they move into the house I shall take a photograph of them dressed in their new pullovers, standing in front of their new house.

Completion sacrifices

In **The Most Beautiful House in the World**, Witold Rybczynski describes how he built his own house. When it was finished he performed the following completion ceremony:

"The wall of bottles was the last to be built. On the oval brown bottom of an Armagnac bottle I inscribed the date, MCMLXXVII, RYBCZYNSKI FECIT, and the names of my co-workers. It was a corner bottle instead of a stone, and we were commoners all; but it would have to do."[40]

Long ago a human was sacrificed when a building was completed because people believed that a building needed a guardian spirit. Sometimes the architect of a new building was the one sacrificed because he was considered the best person to guard his own creation. This practice also assured the uniqueness of a building. When St. Basil's Cathedral in Moscow was completed, the architect was murdered to prevent him from designing a similar or better cathedral in another city. The same story is told of many other churches, both in Russia and elsewhere.

Animal sacrifices eventually replaced human ones. According to one German legend, an architect promises the Devil the soul of the first to enter a church he has built with the Devil's help. The Devil naturally expects a human victim, but he is put off with a wolf, and in a rage he flies up through the roof, leaving a hole that cannot be repaired.

In **The House of the Seven Gables** by Nathaniel Hawthorne, Matthew Maule is executed for the crime of witchcraft, and his land is acquired by his enemy, Colonel Pyncheon, whose death Maule had predicted from the gallows: "God will give him blood to drink!" Over the spot where Matthew Maule's log hut once stood, Colonel Pyncheon builds a grand house, and invites the inhabitants of the local village to attend "a ceremony of consecration, festive as well as religious," to celebrate its completion:

"A prayer and discourse from the Rev. Mr. Higginson, and the outpouring of a psalm from the general throat of the community, was to be made acceptable to the grosser sense by ale, cider, wine, and brandy, in copious effusion, and, as some authorities aver, by an ox, roasted whole, or, at least, by the weight and substance of an ox, in more manageable joints and sirloins. The carcass of a deer, shot within twenty miles, had supplied material for the vast circumference of a pasty. A codfish of sixty pounds, caught in the bay, had been dissolved into the rich liquid of a chowder. The chimney of the new house, in short, belching forth its kitchen smoke, impregnated the whole air with the scent of meats, fowls, and fishes, spicily concocted with odoriferous herbs, and onions in abundance. The mere smell of such festivity, making its way to everybody's nostrils, was at once an invitation and an appetite."[41]

But before the celebration begins, Colonel Pyncheon is found dead with his collar and beard soaked in blood, just as Mathew Maule had predicted. So, in addition to the animals killed for the feast, Colonel Pyncheon was also a completion sacrifice.

Guardian spirits and completion sacrifices are still deep-seated in our consciousness. When an Anglican vicarage or rectory is dedicated, a priest blesses the threshold, the sitting-room, the study, the dining room, the bedrooms, the hall, and the front door of the new house. At the threshold, for example, the priest says: "Grant, O Lord, that all who shall enter this house may enter through Jesus Christ *who is the door,* (author's italics) and entering may find herein Thy presence and peace; through Jesus Christ our Lord. Amen." In other words, not only is God the guardian spirit of the house, but He actually permeates its fabric and structure.

The guardian spirit of Australia's new Parliament House may be the ghost of Sir Robert Menzies (1894-1978), who was Prime Minister of Australia for a total of nineteen years. When the building was opened on May 9, 1988, Prime Minister Bob Hawke said:

"At a time like this each one of us will have some thoughts of the ghosts, or spirits, of the past.... I believe the spirit of Sir Robert Menzies...would be smiling with approval today."[42]

When the Leader of the Opposition was deposed by his Deputy exactly one year after Australia's new Parliament House was opened, some journalists were quick to call the event a completion sacrifice. A report by Mark Harding in the Melbourne *Herald* was headed: "Intrigue and blood-letting christen the new House". Harding went on to say: "No house of politicians is complete without bloodstains."[43]

Wakes

While an opening ceremony celebrates the 'birth' of a building, a wake celebrates the 'death' of a building.[44] It appears that having a wake for a building has become popular in recent years in the United States. For example, the Baker Hotel in Dallas, Texas, which had been the centre of Dallas social life during the 1930's and 1940's, was closed in 1979 and demolished in 1980. Many newspaper reports about the demise of the hotel read in fact like obituaries. One report, which was headed "Baker's demise draws mourners", said the manager of the hotel was "Like the chief mourner at the funeral of a faded old lady,"[45] while another quoted a person as saying "It was like losing a member of the family."[46]

A resolution which in part read, "Several generations of Dallasites feel that this great landmark should not disappear without official recognition of the incomparable role it has played in our lives," was presented to the Dallas County commissioners.[47] In response they declared August 30, 1979 - the last day that the hotel was open for business - "Baker Hotel Day in Dallas County". On that night there was a big party in the hotel where "even the busboys brought Instamatics to record the moment, and the guests' conversations were heavily laced with memory."[48]

In September 1979 everything in the Baker Hotel - linen, crockery, cutlery, furniture and even the floors, walls and ceilings - was put up for sale. People who had honeymooned at the hotel bought the bed on which they had spent their wedding night. After the hotel had been demolished, the place where the debris was dumped was kept secret for fear of souvenir hunters.

The deconsecration ceremony for a church is along similar lines to a wake. When a church is deconsecrated it ceases to be a sacred place, which effectively ends its 'life' as a church.

Conclusion

Altered to suit different buildings, people, places and times, building ceremonies are important for several reasons: they make a place special, which in turn helps to foster a bond between person and place; they permit people to actively participate in the building process; often they are the reactualisation of a primordial event or a sacred history; they are the progenitor of myths and legends; often they constitute the collective memory of the people involved in the building process; and they are powerful design tools.

Writing about the current state of Western building ceremonies in **Space and Place**, Yi-Fu Tuan says:

"Rites and ceremonies that focus on the building activity, which used to be thought of as the creation of a world, have greatly declined so that even in the erection of a large public edifice there remain only the rather wan gestures of laying the foundation-stone and topping."[49]

Western building ceremonies have changed dramatically over the years. Nevertheless, I believe they currently mean more to people than Yi-Fu Tuan suggests here. But his point of view may ultimately prove to be correct if we all are not careful. As far as architects are concerned, I believe their responsibility is clear - architects must be to building ceremonies what geomancers are to feng-shui.

Notes

1. Vitruvius, **The Ten Books on Architecture**, Dover Publications Inc., New York, 1960. [Translated by M.H. Morgan.] p.20.

2. Kidder, T. (1985), **House**, Houghton Mifflin Company, Boston, p.5.

3. *The Sydney Morning Herald,* August 29, 1923.

4. A letter from Alan Tye to Derham Groves, 1983.

5. *The Philadelphia Evening Bulletin,* July 6, 1874.

6. *The Philadelphia Inquirer,* July 6, 1874.

7. Poe, E.A. (1982), **The Complete Tales and Poems of Edgar Allan Poe**, Penguin Books, Harmondsworth, 1984, p.393.

8. ibid., p.394.

9. Eliade, M. (1959), **The Sacred and the Profane**, Harcourt, Brace and World Inc., New York. [Translated by W.R. Trask.] p.54.

10. Brewster, B.H. (1874), **Address by Hon. Benjamin Harris Brewster LL.D., at the laying of the corner stone of the new public buildings, Philadelphia, July 4, 1874**, Henry B. Ashmead, Philadelphia, p.7.

11. ibid., p.14.

12. ibid., p.6.

13. *The Australian,* March 22, 1989.

14. *The Sun,* May 14, 1983.

15. Hersey, G. (1988), **The Lost Meaning of Classical Architecture**, The MIT Press, Cambridge.

16. Kidder, p.141.

17. Doctorow, E.L. (1986), **World's Fair**, Michael Joseph, London, p.270-271.

18. ibid., p.271.

19. Pendray, G.E., *The Story of the Time Capsule, Annual Report, Smithsonian Institution,* 1939, p.539.

20. Fein, H.H. (1938), **The Flying Chinaman**, Alfred A. Knopf, New York, p.26.

21. Speth, G.W., ***Builders' Rites and Ceremonies,*** *Keeble's Gazette,* Margate, 1894, p.22.

22. Doyle, Sir A.C. (1928), **The Complete Sherlock Holmes Short Stories**, John Murray, London, 1953, p.396-417.

23. Seven feet deep and four feet square seems to have been a common size for a death trap. In Edgar Allan Poe's *The Cask of Amontillado,* a man is bricked-up alive in a recess that measures "in depth about four feet, in width three, in height six or seven." Poe, p.277.

24. **Sherlock Holmes Faces Death**, Universal Pictures, USA, 1943.

25. ibid.

26. Ackroyd, P. (1985), **Hawksmoor**, Sphere Books, London, 1986.

27. Dickens, C. (1870), **Edwin Drood & Master Humphrey's Clock**, Chapman & Hall Ltd., Covent Garden, 1907, p.23.

28. Haining, P. (1977), **The Art of Mystery and Detective Stories**, Treasure Press, London, pp. 32 & 54.

29. Frazer, Sir J.G. (1922), **The Golden Bough: A study in Magic and Religion**, The Macmillan Press Ltd., London, 1974, p.154.

30. Ackroyd, pp. 24-25.

31. Scott, J., *Shopkeepers Advertising Novelties, The Strand Magazine,* vol.10, 1895, p.507.

32. Ibsen, H. (1981), **Four Major Plays**, Oxford University Press, Oxford, 1986, p.291. In fact, the master builder does eventually fall to his death while performing the topping ceremony for his own house.

33. Kidder, p.175.

34. Miller, C.H. (1931), **An Early American Home and the Fun We Had Building It**, Thomas Y. Crowell Company, New York, p.216.

35. *The Dallas Times Herald,* October 8, 1986.

36. de Crevecoeur, J.H.St.J. (1782), **Letters from an American Farmer and Sketches of Eighteenth-century America**, Penguin Books, Harmondsworth, 1987, pp.103-104.

37. Rybczynski, W. (1989), **The Most Beautiful House in the World**, Viking, New York.

38. Miller, p.217.

39. *The Age,* May 30, 1899. This was not as dramatic as the opening of the Sargood warehouse in Perth, Western Australia. The Bishop of Perth poured a tin of kerosene over sacks of wood-shavings in the building and set them alight. Fortunately for the reputation of the church, the sprinklers quickly extinguished the blaze.

40. Rybczynski, p.132.

41. Hawthorne, N., **The House of the Seven Gables**, Aerie Books Ltd., USA, 1988, p.7.

42. Speech by the Prime Minister, opening of the new Parliament House, Canberra, May 9, 1988.

43. *The Herald,* May 9, 1989.

44. The word 'wake' also refers to an annual festival held formerly in England in commemoration of the dedication of a parish church, which is quite different from what I mean here.

45. *The Dallas Morning News,* August 1, 1979.

46. *The Dallas Times Herald,* June 30, 1980.

47. *The Dallas Times Herald,* August 28, 1979.

48. *The Dallas Times Herald,* August 31, 1979.

49. Tuan, Y.F. (1977), **Space and Place**, University of Minnesota Press, Minneapolis, p.116.

3. Case study: The feng-shui of 221b Baker Street

221b Baker Street

The University of Minnesota has a huge collection of books and memorabilia about Sherlock Holmes, the famous private detective created by Sir Arthur Conan Doyle. While I was studying at the University of Minnesota in 1984, the curator of the Sherlock Holmes collection asked me to design the interior of 221b Baker Street - the London abode of Sherlock Holmes and his assistant, Dr. Watson, which consists of "a couple of comfortable bedrooms and a single large airy sitting-room"[1] for a display in a shop window.

I made a list of the Baker Street furniture, which is divulged throughout the sixty, original, Sherlock Holmes stories, and arranged it in my design as best I could, since only fragments of rooms are described in the stories. *Figure 74.* But one thing bothered me: people thought about

Figure 74

Figure 75

furniture quite differently during Victorian times than we do today. F. Gordon Roe, for example, remarks on this in **Victorian Furniture**:

"That the Victorians were more 'furniture-conscious' than, for whatever reasons, we have since become is evident in many ways. Dickens, to say nothing of other authors, was continually aware of it, not merely as furniture but as things to be portrayed as vividly as were the characters and the dance through which he led them. Where nowadays furniture is a necessity, to many Victorians it possessed an individuality, almost a mystic quality...."[2]

Roe's remarks are equally true of Sir Arthur Conan Doyle. In *The Musgrave Ritual* for example, Conan Doyle describes some of the trappings in the Baker Street sitting-room so vividly that they seem almost as life-like as Sherlock Holmes himself, while artefacts like the coal-scuttle and the Persian slipper certainly possess a mystic quality, at least for the fans of the great detective:

"Sherlock Holmes was...one of the most untidy men that ever drove a fellow-lodger to distraction.... [He kept] his cigars in the coal-scuttle, his tobacco in the toe-end of a Persian slipper, and his unanswered correspondence transfixed by a jack-knife in the very centre of his wooden mantelpiece.... [He] would sit in an armchair with his hair-trigger and a hundred Boxer cartridges, and proceed to adorn the opposite wall with a patriotic V.R. done in bullet-pocks.... Our chambers were always full of chemicals and of criminal relics which had a way of wandering into unlikely positions, and of turning up in the butter-dish or in even less desirable places."[3] *Figure 75.*

I have mentioned already that during the nineteenth century some people in America and England aligned their houses and furniture with earthly lines of force, believing that this improved their well-being, which sounds curiously like feng-shui. But Roe's comment about furniture possessing a mystic quality for many people during Victorian times, first gave me the idea that perhaps a Victorian approach to furniture placement was closer to a Chinese approach than my own. So, to try to bridge this gap, I asked a number of Chinese geomancers to look at my design of 221b Baker Street, and re-arrange the furniture to reflect the personalities of Holmes and Watson. This also provided an opportunity to directly compare several different feng-shui practices on an equal basis, which I had not seen done before. I belive that 221b Baker Street is an ideal subject for such a study because it is so well known - not only through books about Sherlock Holmes, but also through films, plays and television programmes - that it has become the paradigm of Victorian, middle-class life.

I provided each geomancer with a copy of my design of 221b Baker Street, a map of Baker Street, and four key dates: Sherlock Holmes's birthday (January 6th, 1854), Dr. Watson's birthday (August 7th, 1852), the year that 221b Baker Street was built (1797), and the year that Holmes and Watson began living there (1881).[4]

Three geomancers from Malaysia

I approached three geomancers from Malaysia, but, for various reasons, none of them could evaluate the feng-shui of my design. One geomancer from Kuala Lumpur said he could not get a sufficient feeling for 221b Baker Street from the information I had given him. However, he suggested that Holmes and Watson should keep re-arranging the Baker

Street furniture until they found an arrangement that made them both feel completely at ease. Robert Harbison describes the effects of such a process in **Eccentric Spaces:** "Places thoroughly lived in become internalized in a series of adjustments till they represent a person to himself, a process the critic can try to follow in reverse, deducing the life from the quarters."[5] When it all boils down, perhaps this is what good feng-shui is essentially about - creating an effective bond between person and place. It is certainly evident from the stories that Holmes and Watson have such a bond with 221b Baker Street.

A Taoist priest from Kuala Lumpur, who was also a geomancer, said he required information about the water in the vicinity of 221b Baker Street, as even a sewer pipe under the building might affect its feng-shui. The third geomancer I approached, who came from Penang, refused to participate in the exercise because he assumed that Holmes and Watson were both dead. He did not realise that they transcend the usual three score and ten years of mere mortals!

Evelyn Lip

Evelyn Lip, an architect from Singapore, who has written several books on feng-shui, apparently had no trouble assessing the feng-shui of my design, doing first the rooms together, then the sitting-room alone.[6] To help her locate the qi within 221b Baker Street at any given time, she drew a three-by-three grid over the suite of rooms (A,B,C,1,2,3), and another over just the sitting-room (D,E,F,4,5,6). *Figure 76.* These grids are based on a three-by-three magic square called the 'Luo Shu' (Luo Document), which is believed to have first appeared on the shell of a turtle.[7] The Luo Shu was also regarded as a model of the universe by many Chinese. For example, the nine divisions of the Luo Shu represented such things as the eight points of the compass, with China at the centre; the nine palaces once used by the Chinese emperor throughout the year; and the plan of a traditional Chinese courtyard house.

Analysing the whole of 221b Baker Street, Evelyn Lip said: "Watson's bed should face southeast, which is the luckiest direction for somebody born in 1852. Holmes's bed already faces southwest, which is the luckiest direction for a person born in 1854. Due to the influence of the

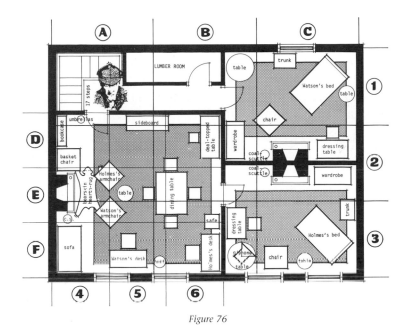

Figure 76

empty house opposite 221b Baker Street, Holmes lived a lonely life, never marrying or having children.

"From 1881 to 1883, B3 was the luckiest area of 221b Baker Street, followed by A3. To bring Holmes and Watson good luck and good health, place their safe and desks within B3. C1, C2 and C3 were unlucky areas from 1881 to 1883. Qi changes location every twenty years, completing a full cycle of change every sixty years. This happened in 1884, and the feng-shui of 221b Baker Street completely changed. B1 became the luckiest area of the house, C2 brought Holmes and Watson wealth and poor health, and C3 brought them good health and no wealth."

Analysing just the sitting-room between 1881 and 1883, Evelyn Lip said: "To bring Holmes and Watson good health, but not wealth, place the sitting-room door within D4. Holmes's bedroom door should be located within E6. To bring Holmes and Watson success, place important pieces of furniture, such as their desks, within F5, which is the luckiest area of the sitting-room. Even though F4 is quite a lucky spot, as long as Watson's desk remains within F4, he will suffer poor health."

Lin Yun

Lin Yun, a leading geomancer from Hong Kong, who practises a style of feng-shui called 'Tibetan black hat feng-shui', also assessed my design of 221b Baker Street. His ideas on feng-shui are the subject of numerous articles in magazines, and two books by Sarah Rossbach.[8] Lin Yun commonly uses three methods to remedy the bad feng-shui of an existing house: (1) The 'connecting qi method' involves tapping the qi far below the earth's surface using a long, hollow pole with a light on top, placed in the ground; (2) The 'balancing method' entails changing an unlucky-shaped plan of a house into a lucky-shaped one by adding a pond or a fountain, for example; (3) The 'outstanding method' involves controlling the flow of qi by, say, hanging a Chinese flute or a wind chime inside a house.

This is what Lin Yun had to say about the feng-shui of 221b Baker Street: "To make 221b Baker Street auspicious, Holmes and Watson should burn nine pieces of dried orange peel, one at a time, inside the house. At the same time, they should make a special hand gesture, recite 'Om Mane Padme Om' nine times,

Figure 77

visualise the smoke from the burning pieces of dried orange peel forcing out the bad qi, and imagine the house bathed in bright sunlight. *Figure 77.* All doors and windows in 221b Baker Street should be protected from malign forces by a special paste made from 'Xiong huang' (yellow bear powder), which many Chinese use to get rid of insects, and ninety-nine drops of strong liquor from a newly opened bottle. Between 11 am and 1 pm, Holmes and Watson should dab this paste above the heads of doors and windows, where doors meet jambs, and where windows meet sills, using only their middle fingers.

"Qi may be good or bad, weak or strong, depending on how it is directed. Ideally, it should be balanced, and flow smoothly. The qi at the top of the stairs, however, is too strong. To disperse it, hang a wind chime from the ceiling between the stairs and the sitting-room door.

"Holmes and Watson should induce qi into the sitting-room by fixing a red thread between the ceiling and the floor in the four corners of the room, which symbolise the connection between heaven and earth. While either Holmes or Watson fixes the threads, the other one should make the special hand gesture, recite 'Om Mane Padme Om' nine times, and visualise the qi flowing into the sitting-room. To help Holmes think clearly and Watson write well, place their desks in the northeast corner of the sitting-room, with enough space behind them so that their chairs can be moved backwards without obstruction. However, their desks should face into the room, not a wall, otherwise the resulting flow of qi will not help them with their work.

"Watson's bed should be placed in the northeast corner of his bedroom, so that his feet point toward the window. His trunk should not be placed at the foot of the bed, because it is bad for his career. To help Holmes think clearly, he should place a double-sided mirror - preferably one that reflects one image larger than the other - under his pillow or mattress. Every morning he should take the mirror outside, clean it, and visualise the qi being reflected by the mirror into his brain." *Figure 78.*

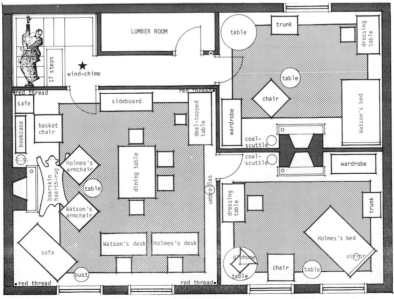

Figure 78

Ma Yan Chow

The final assessment I obtained was done by Ma Yan Chow, another leading geomancer from Hong Kong. He believes that the position of the stove in a house is the most important thing from a feng-shui point of view. He commonly uses three things to improve the feng-shui of an existing house: (1) A bowl of red and/or black- coloured fish to attract money; (2) A round clock with a shiny, gold-coloured face to turn away bad things; (3) A gold-coloured bell, hung by the front door, to welcome good fortune. Ma Yan Chow first identified three paths of good luck running through 221b Baker Street (AB, CD and EF), and placed some important items of furniture on them. *Figure 79.* Paths AB and EF are especially lucky, because each one has an open area at either end.

Here is Ma Yan Chow's assessment of the feng-shui of 221b Baker Street:

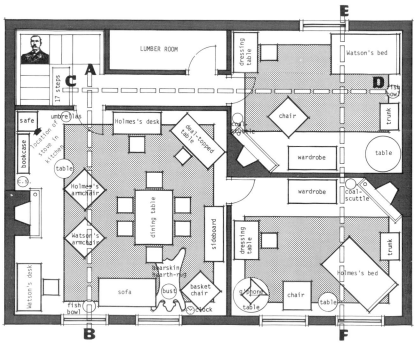

Figure 79

"The Cantonese word for 'six' (luhk), sounds like the English word 'luck'. Therefore, to bring Holmes and Watson luck, place six chairs at the dining table, instead of four. Four is a very unlucky number, because in Cantonese it sounds like 'die' (sei). The words 'fish' and 'surplus' also sound alike in Cantonese (yu); and 'water' (seui) is a common colloquialism for 'money' (chin). Therefore, to attract surplus money into 221b Baker Street, place a bowl containing six red fish in front of the left-hand sitting-room window. Both Holmes' and Watson's armchairs are in good positions because wealth covers both of them (path AB). However, if the bearskin rug remains in front of the fireplace, it will 'eat the money'. It should be put in front of the right-hand, sitting-room window, to act as a guard. Also, place a round clock with a shiny, gold-coloured face on the wall near this window. Holmes's deal-topped table should be put across a corner of the sitting-room, so he faces empty space. According to feng-shui, empty space means long life. Watson's desk is in a good position, but it should be dark-coloured, to correspond with his date of birth.

"Place another bowl containing six red fish in the northeast corner of Watson's bedroom. His bed should not face the door because he may 'easily slip away' (die), and his trunk should not be placed at the foot of his bed. The position of Holmes's bed is excellent: empty space behind the bed means long life. Nothing but Holmes' and Watson's beds should be on path EF."

Conclusion

The assessments put forward by Lip, Yun and Ma do have some points in common. For example, all three are satisfied with the position of Holmes's bed, but are dissatisfied with the position of Watson's bed; Lip and Yun both suggest placing Holmes' and Watson's desks in the northeast corner of the sitting-room; and Yun and Ma both suggest moving the trunk from the foot of Watson's bed. But overall their assessments are quite different. I can suggest a number of possible reasons for this, such as their knowledge of feng-shui was not the same, or each one interpreted the information about 221b Baker Street very differently. However, their differing assessments do not necessarily mean that any of them are wrong. There may be several ways of producing good feng-shui, which is probably also the reason why many people are sceptical about feng-shui.

My final design of 221b Baker Street is based on the assessments by Lip, Yun and Ma. *Figure 80.* I changed the wind chime at the top of the stairs to a hanging lamp, and the red threads in the corners of the sitting-room to decorative, tasselled chords, which both seemed to be more in-keeping with a Victorian interior. Unfortunately my design has not yet been built, so it remains to be seen whether it is a success or not. But I do think that it was very helpful to be guided by three people who are probably more furniture-conscious than most people were during Victorian times.

Figure 80

Notes

1. Doyle, Sir A.C. (1929), **The Sherlock Holmes Long Stories**, John Murray, London, 1952, p.14.

2. Roe, F.G., **Victorian Furniture**, Phoenix House Limited, London, 1952, p.106.

3. Doyle, Sir A.C. (1928), **The Complete Sherlock Holmes Short Stories**, John Murray, London, 1953, p.396.

4. Sherlock Holmes and Dr. Watson have been scrutinized like real people. William S. Baring-Gould suggested that January 6th, 1854, was Holmes's birthday; August 7th, 1852, was Watson's birthday; and 1881 was the year that they both began living at 221b Baker Street [Baring-Gould, W.S. (1962), **Sherlock Holmes: A Biography of the World's First Consulting Detective**, Rupert Hart-Davis, London, pp.250 and 253]. Number 111 Baker Street, the house identified by Dr. Gray Chandler Briggs as 221b, first appeared in the rate books in 1797 [Starrett, V. (1933), **The Private Life of Sherlock Holmes**, The Macmillan Company, New York, pp.60-61].

5. Harbison, R. (1977), **Eccentric Spaces**, Martin Secker & Warburg Limited, London, 1989, p.22.

6. Lip, E. (1979), **Chinese Geomancy**, Times Books International, Singapore; and (1986), **Feng Shui for the Home**, Times Books International, Singapore.

7. Plastromancy, which involves interpreting cracks induced by fire on a turtle's shell, was a common form of divination in ancient China.

8. Rossbach, S. (1983), **Feng Shui: The Chinese Art of Placement**, E.P. Dutton Inc., New York; and (1987), **Interior Design with Feng Shui**, Century Hutchinson Ltd., Covent Garden.

4. Case study: The Hermann monument

Introduction

Architects once regarded building ceremonies as their reponsibility. Nowadays, however, architects are seldom masters of ceremonies; they often overlook the place-making value of building ceremonies, and consequently opportunities are lost. But I believe an architect should still be a master of ceremonies, like Julius Berndt.

He designed a monument dedicated to the German hero 'Hermann the War Man' which is located in New Ulm, Minnesota. *Figure 81.* It was commissioned by a society called the Sons of Hermann, which based its rituals on the Hermann legend. The monument is a reminder of Julius Berndt's skill, not only as a designer, but also as a master of ceremonies. Under his direction, building ceremonies transformed the site of the monument into a magical space and brought the Hermann legend to life.

Background

To make the frontiers of their empire secure, the Romans advanced into northwestern Germany and conquered the tribes living between the Rhine and the Weser. Hermann, the chief of the Cherusci tribe, was taken prisoner and sent to Rome. He learned Latin, became a Roman citizen, and served in the Roman army. After a time he returned to Germany and resumed his position as tribal chief. The Romans believed Hermann was their ally, but all along he was plotting to liberate his people from Roman rule. In 9 A.D. the Roman army was ambushed in the Teutoberg forest by Hermann and his followers. After three days of fierce fighting the Roman army was defeated.

In 1862 the little town of New Ulm, Minnesota, was violently attacked by the Sioux and nearly destroyed. "So complete was the work of the

Figure 81

savages," writes Edward D. Neill in the **History of the Minnesota Valley**, "that when all was again quiet there were only thirty buildings left standing that could be occupied."[1]

The Hermann monument commemmorates both of these battles which, on the surface, appear to be totally unconnected. However, at the unveiling of the monument in 1897, the national leader of the Sons of Herman declared:

"We are now in the friendly and beautiful city of New Ulm at the foot of the monument, and well might the stranger ask why this monument, fit by reason of its grandeur to adorn the finest park in the metropolis of America, should have been erected in the far west. The question is quite in order. The answer is easy.

"In Germany you will find a monument to Hermann erected and dedicated during the rule of Kaiser Wilhelm, but not at Cologne, or Dresden or Munich. On the contrary, it adorns the little village of Detmold in the vicinity of which Hermann won his greatest battle.

"Now for similar reasons New Ulm has been selected as the site for this grand statue. Here thirty-five years ago the Germans waged war with the savage and bloodthirsty Indians. Here the German was compelled to defend his dear ones and his home against a cruel and inhuman enemy - the relentless Sioux."[2]

Furthermore, a report in the *St. Paul Dispatch* said New Ulm had "passed through bloody ordeals in the early days of her existence, and *her own Hermanns* (author's italics) saved the city from utter destruction at the hands of relentless foes."[3]

Site selection

Although a committee was appointed to select a site for the Hermann monument in New Ulm, it appears that the final decision was made by Julius Berndt. The site which he chose is on a bluff at the southwestern edge of the city- the place where the Sioux launched their attack on New Ulm in 1862. The site was sacred in other respects too. A report in the *New Ulm Review* said it had been "formed by nature into a beautiful park,

Figure 82

irrigated by springs and dotted with numerous trees, conspicuous among them the knotty oak, the laurel of the Germans. No better place could have been selected for the site of the monument...."[4]

The Sons of Hermann met on the vacant site of the monument, received the deeds for the land, and 'christened' the site 'Hermann's Heights'. "The christening was performed with all due solemnity...."[5] reported the *New Ulm Review. Figure 82.* In **The Idea of a Town**, Josheph Rykwert describes the founding of the site of a new town in ancient Rome. But he could just as easily be describing the founding of the site of the Hermann monument in New Ulm: "The [Sons of Hermann] had taken possession of the site...expelled such previous ghostly inhabitants as were unfriendly...given it a name and invoked a protecting deity...."[6]

The foundation-stone ceremony

I believe a foundation-stone ceremony should enshrine at least two ideas: firstly, a foundation-stone is laid at the centre of the world; and secondly, the foundation deposits buried under a foundation-stone

Figure 83

serve as the spirit of a building. Both of these ideas were evident in the foundation-stone ceremony of the Hermann monument.

People used to march to a foundation-stone ceremony, which strengthened the idea that a foundation-stone was laid at the centre of the world. In the case of the Hermann monument, the Sons of Hermann marched from New Ulm to Hermann's Heights to attend the monument's foundation-stone ceremony. On Centre Street they passed through a ceremonial arch which Julius Berndt had designed and built especially for the occasion. *Figure 83.* All along the route of the procession the streets and buildings were decorated with banners, bunting, evergreen wreaths, flags, garlands of leaves, and lanterns. "New Ulm never before presented a grander or more festive appearance and was quite overpowered by the many guests that thronged her streets,"[7] reported the *New Ulm Review.*

Usually an important person lays a foundation-stone at an auspicious time, which adds to the importance of the event. The important person's speech may also help to reinforce the idea that a foundation-stone is laid at the centre of the world. In the case of the Hermann monument, the national leader of the Sons of Hermann laid the monument's foundation-stone on June 24, 1888, during the annual 'Turnfest' in New Ulm. After the national leader of the Sons of Hermann had laid the foundation-stone, he declared:

"May future years, when all of us have passed away, witness this monument as the centre, about which the Sons of Hermann a hundred-thousand strong will gather, ever a protector for the glorious, happy freedom of this country."[8]

In other words, the Hermann monument was located at the centre of the world of the Sons of Hermann, and it would last forever.

The foundation deposits buried under a foundation-stone constitute the spirit of a buiding. In the case of the Hermann monument, seventy-eight foundation deposits which reflected the ideals of the Sons of Hermann were placed in a tin box and buried beneath the monument's foundation-stone. Among the foundation deposits was a photograph of Julius Berndt, a photograph of the Hermann monument in Germany, a sketch of New Ulm, a list of the volunteers who defended New Ulm between 1861 and 1865, and a copy of the **Outbreak of the Sioux Indians** by Captain Jacob Nix.

At a traditional German house- or barn-raising, the master builder often commemorated the occasion by proposing a toast and flinging his glass or bottle at the frame of the building under construction. If the vessel did not break, however, the owner of the building was supposed to die soon afterwards. So, one way or another, a sacrifice was part of the event. It appears that something similar occurred at the foundation-stone ceremony of the Hermann monument. When the monument was restored in 1972, workmen found a broken wine glass lying on top of the box containing the foundation deposits.

When the box was opened, workmen discovered that moisture had penetrated the box and damaged some of the foundation deposits inside. The undamaged foundation deposits, together with some new ones, were placed in a different container and re-buried under the monument's foundation-stone. So, the Hermann monument was not only restored physically, but also spiritually.

The opening ceremony

The Hermann monument was opened by the Governor of Minnesota on September 25, 1897, during the national convention of the Sons of Hermann in New Ulm. In summing up the monument's opening ceremony, a report in the *Sunday Times* said: "Not since the Indian outbreak thirty-five years ago has the city of New Ulm experienced such excitement...."[9]

Figure 84

The celebrations began with a parade through the streets of New Ulm which ended at Hermann's Heights. Julius Berndt had designed and built a ceremonial arch which spanned the street leading to the monument, besides many of the floats in the parade. Some of the floats represented Columbia, Liberty, a Roman chariot, and Hermann and his men. *Figure 84*. A report in the *St. Paul Dispatch* said the parade commemorated "...all the scenes of the battle of Hermann and of the many battles the Germans of New Ulm have fought."[10]

The opening ceremony of the Hermann monument actualized Hermann's battle against the Romans, which enabled the Sons of Hermann to travel backwards in time and become contemporary with their hero. Discussing this phenomenon in general in **The Sacred and the Profane**, Mircea Eliade writes: "This faithful repetition of divine models has a two-fold result: (i) by imitating the gods, man remains in the sacred, hence in reality; (ii) by continuous reactualization of paradigmatic divine gestures, the world is sanctified."[11]

A talisman

The Hermann monument protected New Ulm from harm. If the city had been attacked again, it would have been defended from the monument which had a weapons depository inside the dome, similar to a Norman 'keep' or 'place of defence'. Furthermore, like a talisman, the giant image of 'Hermann the War Man' would have protected and strengthened the defenders of the city. *Figure 85.*

Figure 85

Conclusion

Feng-shui is fascinating - to Westerners especially - because it is dynamic in character, a living tradition which is taken very seriously by many Chinese people.

Some may say that, currently, there is nothing like feng-shui in Western culture. I hope this book has shown that this is not the case. Western building ceremonies relating to turning the first sod, laying a foundation-stone, completing the roof-framing and opening a new building are quite similar to feng-shui in form and function.

What Western culture does lack is a person like a geomancer. However, if architects were responsible for building ceremonies, as they used to be, this void would be filled. Not only would this benefit architects, but, more importantly, the whole community as well.

Notes

1. Neill, E.D. (1882), **History of the Minnesota Valley**, North Star Publishing Company, Minneapolis, p.707.

2. *New Ulm Review,* September 29, 1897.

3. *St. Paul Dispatch,* September 20, 1897.

4. *New Ulm Review,* May 23, 1888.

5. *New Ulm Review,* September 9, 1885.

6. Rykwert, J. (1976), **The Idea of a Town: The Anthropology of Urban Form in Rome, Italy and the Ancient World**, The MIT Press, Cambridge, 1988, pp.65-66.

7. *New Ulm Review,* June 27, 1888.

8. ibid.

9. *Sunday Times,* September 26, 1897.

10. *St. Paul Dispatch,* September 20, 1897.

11. Eliade, M. (1959), **The Sacred and the Profane**, Harcourt, Brace and World Inc., New York. [Translated by W.R. Trask.] p.99.

Afterword

Today, in an increasingly abstract and intangible world characterised by neither belief nor spiritual values, we need to create a personally strong sense of place, an anchor to the soil.

Architecture creates place by enclosing or bounding space, and confirms it through the inertia of statics. All successful architecture roots and holds a building in place, to the satisfaction of both our eyes and our emotions.

Events now flash everywhere by satellite, and this is causing a profound change in our social habits. Human behaviour was once specific to place and situation. People behaved one way in private and another in public; one way in front of children and another with adults. Television, the people's media, has altered our assumptions. It is not only a public medium but also an intimate one, bringing the outside world into the living room, to be watched by child and adult alike.

Distinctions between previously well-understood situations are blurred and we have less well-defined roles to play. We dress and act casually in public, treat children as ill-mannered adults, judge public figures on performance and personal presentation rather than on intelligence and ideas. An important dimension to our sense of place has been eroded; some of the behavioural clues have gone missing. The boundaries of our spatial world are no longer clear.

The very fluidity of the television media is loosening our grip on place, while homogenising our overall understanding of the world. Modern technology and its ethos have recast the world. It could be argued that the electronic media are etherealising both the public and the private realm so that neither is rooted any longer in place or space. In the midst of the numbing experience, architecture needs to provide long term meaning in the face of short term change. In some circles this is viewed as a provocative idea.

If we are to sustain a sense of place in our cities, or more to the point, in the buildings in which we live and work, then technology must be allocated its proper role. Architecture both exploits and is serviced by technology, but it also transcends it, and in some very important ways is profoundly anti-technological in its values. The general public craves architecture that establishes place and satisfies our aspirations for permanence and survival. Nowadays, in social terms, the language of patriotism may not be fashionable, but the appetite for 'roots' - albeit often make-believe ones - is unappeasable.

In a world without clearly understood roots, it is little wonder that many of us have anxieties about what is real. This disturbing state of affairs can only be reinforced by the electronic revolution. Increasing numbers work in a world of abstract intangibles that are flashed upon screens. Their daily reality is made up of images, figures, numbers and diagrams. The 'intelligent' buildings in which the work is pursued is often simply compartments of highly serviced, environmentally neutral space, with tinted windows, designer lighting and power, talking elevators, variable volume air-conditioning, central monitoring computers, key-card security and ergonomic furniture. At home, the phantasy world of electronic entertainment and instant replay continue this erosion of our awareness of the outside world. This behaviour nullifies large areas of our potential, human, real, sensual experience.

In a world of increasing intangibility and abstractions, the role of the architect should be more than ever a shaman of space, a diviner of place, the guardian of deeply human truth. Place is not simply grounded in all the specifics of a situation but engages with social protocols. It should be rich in inward experience, not merely popularism.

Mr. Groves, himself an architect, has written a book that reveals some of the various strategies and public rituals employed by ancient civilisations and our own to confirm ongoing relationships with the inward human experience of place. To fulfill our future lives, myths of construction need to be consciously located at the centre stage of present-day building practice. The enactment of myths contributes to revelation.

Peter Corrigan
Architect
Edmond & Corrigan Pty Ltd
1991

Bibliography

ACROYD, P. (1986), **Hawksmoor**, Sphere Books, London, 1986.

ARAGON, L. (1971), **Paris Peasant**, Picador, London, 1980. [Translated by S.W. Taylor.]

BAKER, H. (1979), **Ancestral Images: A Hong Kong Album**, South China Morning Post Limited, Hong Kong.

BAKER, H. (1980), **More Ancestral Images: A Second Hong Kong Album**, South China Morning Post Limited, Hong Kong.

BAKER, H. (1981), **Ancestral Images Again: A Third Hong Kong Album**, South China Morning Post Limited, Hong Kong.

BALL, J.D. (1903), **Things Chinese**, Graham Brash, Singapore 1989.

BARING-GOULD, S., **Germany**, T. Fisher Unwin, London, 1889.

BARING-GOULD, S., *On Foundations, Murray's Magazine,* 1887.

BARING-GOULD, S., *On Gables, Murray's Magazine,* 1887.

BARING-GOULD, W.S. (1962), **Sherlock Holmes: A Biography of the World's First Consulting Detective**, Rupert Hart-Davis, London.

BLOOMFIELD, F. (1983), **The Book of Chinese Beliefs: A Journey into the Chinese Inner World**, Ballantine Books, New York, 1989.

BLOODWORTH, D. (1966), **The Chinese Looking Glass**, Farrar Straus Giroux, New York, 1980.

BOSE, N.K. (1932), **Canons of Orissan Architecture: Based on Texts from the Bhuvana-pradipa and Silpa-sastra or Silpa-pothi**, Chatterjee, Calcutta.

BREWSTER, B.H. (1874), **Address by Hon. Benjamin Harris Brewster, LL.D., at the Laying of the Corner Stone of the New Public Buildings, Philadelphia, July 4, 1874**, Henry B. Ashmead, Philadelphia.

BRIGGS, A. (1965), **Victorian Cities**, Odham Books, London.

BROWN, R.B. [editor] (1980), **Rituals and Ceremonies in Popular Culture**, Bowling Green University Popular Press, Bowling Green.

BURKHARDT, V.R. (1953), **Chinese Creeds and Customs**, South China Morning Post Ltd., Hong Kong, 1982.

CALDWELL, J.L., *Notes on the Ceremonial Procedure for Formally Laying a Foundation Stone, RIBA Journal,* October 1961.

CHAMBERS, Sir W. (1757), **Designs of Chinese Buildings, Furniture, Dresses, Machines and Utensils,** Arno Press Inc., New York, 1980.

CHAPMAN, A., ***Tai Po Tsai Burial Ground,*** *Landscape Australia,* August 1984.

CHUA-EOAN, H.G., ***How to Keep the Dragons Happy,*** *Time,* June 22, 1987.

CONNER, P. (1979), **Oriental Architecture in the West,** Thames and Hudson Ltd., London.

CRITCHLOW, K., *Nike: The Siting of a Japanese Rural House,* in OLIVER, P. [editor] (1975), **Shelter, Sign and Symbol,** Barrie & Jenkins, London.

DANIELLI, M., ***The "Mpanandro" (Maker of Days) of Imerina, Madagascar,*** *Folklore,* December 1949.

DANIELLI, M., ***The Geomancer in China, with some Reference to Geomancy as Observed in Madagascar,*** *Folklore,* 96, 1952.

de Crevecoeur, J.H.St.J. (1782), **Letters from an American Farmer and Sketches of Eighteenth-century America,** Penguin Books Ltd., Harmondsworth, 1987.

DeGROOT, J.J.M. (1897), **The Religious System of China,** Brill, Leiden.

DICKENS, C. (1870), **Edwin Drood & Master Humphrey's Clock,** Chapman & Hall Ltd., Covent Garden, 1907.

DOCTOROW, E.L. (1986), **World's Fair,** Michael Joseph, London.

DORE, H. (1914-1929), **Researches into Chinese Superstitions,** T'usewei Printing Press, Shanghai. [Translated by M. Kennelly.]

DOYLE, Sir A.C. (1928), **The Complete Sherlock Holmes Short Stories,** John Murray, London, 1953.

DOYLE, Sir A.C. (1929), **The Sherlock Holmes Long Stories,** John Murray, London, 1952.

EITEL, E.J. (1873), **Feng-shui: The Science of Sacred Landscape in Old China,** Graham Brash, Singapore, 1985.

ELIADE, M. (1959), **The Sacred and the Profane,** Harcourt, Brace and World Inc., New York. [Translated by W. R. Trask.]

FEIN, H.H. (1938), **The Flying Chinaman,** Alfred A. Knopf, New York.

FEUCHTWANG, S.D.R. (1974), **An Anthropological Analysis of Chinese Geomancy,** Southern Materials Centre, Inc., Taipei.

FITZGERALD, A. (1983), **Canberra and the New Parliament House,** Lansdowne Press, Sydney.

FRAZER, Sir J.G. (1922), **The Golden Bough: A study in Magic and Religion**, The Macmillan Press Ltd., London, 1974.

FREEDMAN, M., *Geomancy, Proceedings of the Royal Anthropological Institute of Great Britain and Ireland,* 1968.

FRITSCHE, L.A. (1916), **History of Brown County, Minnesota**, vol.III, B.F. Brown, Indianapolis.

GIBBS, P. (1987), **Building the Malay House**, Oxford University Press, Singapore.

GITTINS, J. (1981), **The Diggers from China**, Quartet Books, Melbourne.

GROVES, D., *Dear Richard Thorpe, Transition,* March 1981.

HAINING, P. (1977), **The Art of Mystery and Detective Stories**, Treasure Press, London.

HARBISON, R. (1977), **Eccentric Spaces**, Martin Secker & Warburg Limited, London, 1989.

HAWTHORNE, N., **The House of the Seven Gables**, Aerie Books Ltd., USA, 1988.

HETTEL, J.N., *The Cornerstone, Journal of the AIA,* November 1952.

HERSEY, G. (1988), **The Lost Meaning of Classical Architecture**, The MIT Press, Cambridge.

HOCH, E.D., *The Spy and the Geomancers, Ellery Queen's Mystery Magazine,* October 1989.

IBSEN, H. (1981), **Four Major Plays**, Oxford University Press, Oxford, 1986.

JONES, B.E. (1950), **Freemasons' Guide and Compendium**, George G. Harran & Co. Ltd., London.

JONSON, B., **The Alchemist**, Cambridge University Press, Cambridge, 1967. [Edited by J.B. Steane.]

KHIAT, T.K., *Sailing with the Wind: Feng Shui, Today,* August 12, 1984.

KIDDER, T. (1985), **House**, Houghton Mifflin Company, Boston.

KIGHTLY, C. (1987), **The Perpetual Almanac of Folklore**, Thames and Hudson, London.

LAI, C.Y.D., *A Feng Shui Model as a Location Index, Annals of the Association of American Geographers,* December 1974.

LANG, S., and Pevsner, N., *Sir William Temple and Sharawaggi, Architectural Review,* 16, 1949.

LEGGE, J., trans. (1882) **The I Ching - The Book of China**, Graham Brash, Singapore, 1990.

LETHABY, W.R. (1891), **Architecture, Mysticism and Myth**, The Architecture Press Ltd., London, 1974.

L_VI-STRAUSS, C. (1955), **Tristes Tropiques**, Penguin Books Ltd., Harmondsworth, 1978. [Translated by J. and D. Weightman.]

LIP, E. (1979), **Chinese Geomancy**, Times Books International, Singapore.

LIP, E. (1983), **Chinese Temple Architecture in Singapore**, Singapore University Press, Singapore.

LIP, E. (1986), **Feng Shui for the Home**, Times Books International, Singapore.

LIP, E., *Planning Buildings with Reference to Feng Shui*, Architecture Australia, March 1987.

LONG, A. (1972), **The Pennsylvania Family Farm**, vol.VI, Pennsylvania German Society, Breinigsville.

MARQUAND, J.P. (1936), **Thank You Mr. Moto**, Bestseller Library, number 12, New York.

MERRICK, L., **Conrad in Quest of his Youth**, Hodder & Stoughton, London. [Introduction by J.M. Barrie.]

MICHELL, J. (1969), **The New View over Atlantis**, Harper and Row, San Francisco, 1983.

MICHELL, J. (1975), **The Earth Spirit: Its Ways, Shrines and Mysteries**, Crossroad, New York.

MIDDLEBROOK, S.M., *Ceremonial Opening of a New Chinese Temple at Kandang, Malacca, in December, 1938 Journal of the Malayan Branch of the Royal Asiatic Society*, vol.XVII, part I, 1939.

MILLER, C.H. (1931), **An Early American Home and the Fun We Had Building It**, Thomas Y. Crowell Company, New York.

MORRIS, Rev. T.M. (1892), **A Winter in North China**, Fleming H. Revell Company, New York.

MORRISON, G.E. (1895), **An Australian in China**, Horace Cox, London.

NEILL, E.D. (1882), **History of the Minnesota Valley**, North Star Publishing Company, Minneapolis.

PALMER, M. [editor and translator] **T'ung sh'u**, Century Hutchinson Ltd., London, 1986.

PENDRAY, G.E., *The Story of the Time Capsule*, Annual Report Smithsonian Institution, 1939.

PENNICK, N., (1979), **The Ancient Science of Geomancy**, Thames and Hudson, London.

PENNICK, N. (1986), **Skulls, Cats and Witch Bottles**, Nigel Pennick Editions, Cambridge.

PENNICK, N. (1987), **Earth Harmony**, Century Hutchinson Ltd., London.

POE, E.A. (1982), **The Complete Tales and Poems of Edgar Allan Poe**, Penguin Books Ltd., Harmondsworth, 1984.

POLO, M., **The Travels**, Penguin Books Ltd., Harmondsworth, 1978. [Translated by R. Lantham.]

QUEEN, E. (1934), **The Chinese Orange Mystery**, Penguin Books Ltd., Harmondsworth, 1956.

RAPOPORT, A. (1969), **House Form and Culture**, Prentice-Hall Inc., Englewood Cliffs.

RAY, A. (1964), **Villages, Towns and Secular Buildings in Ancient India, c.150 B.C. - c.350 A.D.**, Firma K.L. Mukhopadhyay, Calcutta.

RICHARDS, A. [editor] **The Sea Dyaks and Other Races of Sarawak: Contributions to the *Sarawak Gazettete* between 1888 and 1930**, Borneo Literature Bureau, Kuching, 1977.

ROE, F.G. (1952), **Victorian Furniture**, Phoenix House Limited, London.

ROSSBACH, S. (1983), **Feng Shui: The Chinese Art of Placement**, E.P. Dutton Inc., New York.

ROSSBACH, S. (1987), **Interior Design with Feng Shui**, Century Hutchinson Ltd., Covent Garden.

ROSSI, A. (1982), **The Architecture of the City**, The MIT Press, Cambridge.

RUSHEN, J., *Folklore and Witchcraft in Tudor and Stuart England, Popular Archaeology*, April 1984.

RYBCZYNSKI, W. (1989), **The Most Beautiful House in the World**, Viking, New York.

RYKWERT, J. (1976), **The Idea of a Town: The Anthropology of Urban Form in Rome, Italy and the Ancient World**, The MIT Press, Cambridge, 1988.

SCOTT, J., *Shopkeepers' Advertising Novelties, The Strand Magazine,* vol.10, 1895.

SHAW, W. (1975), **Aspects of Malaysian Magic**, Yau Seng Press, Kuala Lumpur.

SINCLAIR, I. (1975), **Lud Heat**, Albion Village Press, London.

SKINNER, S. (1982), **The Living Earth Manual of Feng-shui: Chinese Geomancy**, Routledge & Kegan Paul, London and Graham Brash, Singapore, 1983.

SPETH, G.W., *Builders' Rites and Ceremonies, Keeble's Gazette,* Margate, 1894.

STACK, R.D., *Magic and Space, Annals of the Association of American Geographers,* June 1976.

STARRETT, V. (1933), **The Private Life of Sherlock Holmes**, The Macmillan Company, New York.

STILGOE, J.R. (1982), **Common Landscape of America, 1580 to 1845**, Yale University Press, New Haven.

STIRLING, W.G., *Chinese Divining Blocks and the "Pat Kwa" or Eight-sided Diagram with Text Figures, Journal of the Malayan Branch of the Royal Asiatic Society,* vol.II, 1924.

TOPLEY, M., *Paper Charms and Prayer Sheets as Adjuncts to Chinese Worship, Journal of the Malayan Branch of the Royal Asiatic Society,* vol.XXVI, part I, 1953.

TUAN, Y.F. (1974), **Topophilia: A study of Environmental Perception, Attitudes and Values**, Prentice-Hall Inc., Englewood Cliffs.

TUAN, Y.F. (1977), **Space and Place**, University of Minnesota Press, Minneapolis.

TUAN, Y.F. (1979), **Landscapes of Fear**, University of Minnesota Press, Minneapolis.

TURNER, F. S., *Feng-shui, Cornhill Magazine,* 29, 1874.

UNDERWOOD, G. (1972), **The Pattern of the Past**, Abacus, London.

VITRUVIUS, **The Ten Books on Architecture**, Dover Publications Inc., New York, 1960. [Translated by M.H. Morgan.]

WALTERS, D. (1988), **Feng Shui - The Chinese Art of Designing a harmonious Environment**, Simon & Schuster Inc., New York. H

WATKINS, A. (1925), **The Old Straight Track**, Sphere Books, London, 1980.

WU, C.T., **The Scholars**, Foreign Languages Press, Peking, 1983. [Translated by Yang Hsien-Yi and G. Yang.]

WU, N.I. (1963), **Chinese & Indian Architecture**, Studio Vista Limited, London, 1968.

YANG, M.C. (1945), **A Chinese village: Taitou, Shantung Province**, Columbia University Press, New York, 1965.

YEE, C. (1950), **The Silent Traveller in New York**, Meuthuen & Co. Ltd., London.

Illustration Credits

Figure

1. Calligraphy by Khoo Lip Chee

2. After Skinner, Table 5, pp.66-67

3. Drawing by Danny Gu Zhong Liang (after WU, Figure 136, unpaginated)

4. Drawing by Danny Gu Zhong Liang (after LAI, Figure 2, p.509)

5. Photograph by Damian Curry

6. The Research Institute of Surveying and Mapping

24. 26. 28. Drawings by Danny Gu Zhong Liang

30. 31. 32. 33. Model by David Gundy, photographs by Damian Curry

34. 35. Model by Wang Ko Chung, photographs by Damian Curry

38. Drawing by Danny Gu Zhong Liang (after PDCM)

39. Foster Associates

40. Model by Christopher Lim Meng How, photograph by Damian Curry

41. Model by Stephen Lightbody, photo by Damian Curry

42. Model by Roland Thompson, photo by Damian Curry

49. Based on photograph from *The Sydney Morning Herald,* August 31, 1923, p.10

50. Photo by Carol Urness

51. Allgood

52. National Library of Australia

54. National Aeronautics and Space Administration

55. Photo by Chris Ellis

56. View Productions, photo by Ken Stepnell

57. *The Australian*, March 22, 1989, p.1, cartoon by Mark Lynch

58. Steel Reinforcement Promotion Group

59. Drawing by Danny Gu Zhong Liang

60. PENDRAY, Figure 1, p.535

61. *The Strand Magazine*, vol.V, 1893, drawing by Sidney Paget

62. Drawing by Danny Gu Zhong Liang (after HAINING, p.32)

63. SCOTT, Figure 5, p.507

65. 68. Drawings by Danny Gu Zhong Liang

73. Knitting by Ethel Groves

75. Rare Books and Special Collections, University of Minnesota

81. *New Ulm Review*, May 23, 1888

82. 83. 84. 85. Brown County Historical Society